SOCIETY AND SOCIAL POLICY:
THEORETICAL PERSPECTIVES
ON WELFARE

Society and Social Policy: Theoretical Perspectives on Welfare

RAMESH MISHRA

*Department of Social Studies,
Portsmouth Polytechnic*

First published 1977 by
THE MACMILLAN PRESS LTD
London and Basingstoke
Associated companies in Delhi Dublin
Hong Kong Johannesburg Lagos Melbourne
New York Singapore and Tokyo

ISBN 0 333 21504 4 (hard cover)
0 333 21505 2 (paper cover)

Printed in Great Britain by
UNWIN BROTHERS LIMITED
The Gresham Press, Old Woking, Surrey
A member of the Staples Printing Group

2 0 JAN 1978

To E. H. Crawford

Contents

other hand, the view that generalisations cannot be made until an exhaustive body of data has been accumulated seems to me both unrealistic and mistaken. Firstly, we may never be able to reach the ideal state of affairs concerning data. Second, and more important, the work of generalising, 'model-building', theorising and so on must go hand in hand with the accumulation of facts. Indeed, one cannot even gather facts meaningfully without having some sort of a theory (however implicit) or general idea of what to look for. The important point, then, is not to shy away from generalisations but to treat them as working hypotheses which need to be tested against evidence. The material in Part 2 should be seen largely in these terms.

So far we have used the term social policy without really defining it. What exactly is our field of inquiry? Social policy can be defined in relatively narrow or wide terms. There is nothing intrinsically right or wrong about such definitions except that the definition adopted should be appropriate to the task in hand. The concerns of this book – for example, the examination of theories of the relation between society and social policy – demand a broad definition of the subject matter. As used here the term refers, in a generic sense, to the aims and objectives of social action concerning needs as well as to the structural patterns or arrangements through which needs are met. Our definition is not restricted to government action and arrangements concerning needs (we use the term social services for this) nor indeed to the context of industrial societies. Perhaps some such term as the institution of welfare or welfare policy expresses our meaning better. Indeed, in this book the terms welfare and social welfare have been used more or less interchangeably with the term social policy throughout. The reasons for this are not only stylistic. In pre-industrial – for example, tribal – societies needs may be met largely through traditional rules of reciprocity. These arrangements have broadly the same end in view as social policy in industrial societies. But clearly the term policy, which suggests a deliberateness and a rational matching of ends and means, would be inappropriate in this context: welfare seems more apt. But this is largely a question of the appropriate term. More important, and perhaps open to objection, is the broad (and hence somewhat elusive) view of social policy adopted here. One reason for this is that too specific a view of the subject matter carries the risk of excluding certain relevant perspectives altogether simply by virtue of definition. In a book concerned with differing approaches to social policy we naturally wish to avoid this, preferring to err on the side of a wide rather than a narrow definition. Briefly, then, our interest lies in those social arrangements, patterns and mechanisms that are typically concerned with the distribution of resources in accordance with some criterion of need. We cannot be more specific than this since one of the main aims of the book is to look at the nature and meaning of welfare within a wide societal perspective. Thus the notion of welfare used here is more akin to broad social categories like religion, education, kinship or politics than to specific social organisations like the social services. The student of welfare cannot equate his subject matter with government policy in Britain any more than, say, the student of religion can equate his with the problems and policies of the Church of England. However, if in this respect the approach adopted here is unconventional in another respect it is fully conformist. (It did not seem either desirable or practicable to break away from tradition altogether.) Thus our discussion often centres around those needs and services (education, health, income security and housing but not transport, gas, electricity and so on) that have come to be recognised as the subject matter of social policy. This is particularly true of Part 2 of the book, which is empirical and focused on the social services.

Lastly, a word about the disciplinary orientation of this book: it is sociological. To say this is to warn the lay reader about jargon: it has been kept to a minimum. But a sociological text (let alone a psychology or economics text for undergraduates) cannot be expected to read like a novel – written in 'plain' English. Concepts are necessary for the understanding of social reality whose complexity cannot be adequately expressed in everyday language. Sociology, like economics, history, philosophy and others, is one of the many disciplines that contribute (or should contribute) to the study of social policy. What is offered here is one such contribution. The relevance of this book to the practical issues of policy is of course indirect. I hope this will not deter the practically minded student from looking at the relation between policy and society. I hope too that the book will stimulate the sociologists' interest in social policy. Indeed, it is also meant as a bridge between sociology and social administration in the belief that more traffic should flow in both directions between these two territories.

Part 1

Approaches to Welfare

an impressive empirical tradition while lacking any systematic body of explanatory theory'.[1] Indeed, this is one of the main differences between social administration and the other perspectives outlined in this book. Whereas the latter are primarily attempts to generalise about the nature and development of welfare (albeit at varying levels of generality and scope), social administration eschews general explanations and theories.

In a perceptive study of the relation between social theory and the making and analysis of social policy in Britain, Pinker explains this in terms of the origins of social administration as a social activity – its development as a 'makeshift rearguard action against the authoritative prescriptions of certain forms of normative theory, which sought to explain and justify, a new kind of competitive and industrial social order'.[2] In a nutshell, against the elegant but misleading theories of economic and social *laissez-faire* the reformers used facts – evidence rather than counter-theory – as their main weapon. Hence the intellectual contribution of social administration took the form of the refutation of normative theory by reference to evidence. Pinker finds it 'tempting' to explain 'the continuing resistance of the discipline to theory' in terms of these origins. Theory is mistrusted since the very history of social administration is 'the record of an arduous campaign against the social consequences of theory, and especially the normative theory of political economy'.[3] While this is an interesting and plausible explanation, it is not entirely convincing. For one thing it is somewhat fanciful to suggest that there is anything like a 'continuing resistance' to theory among the practitioners of social administration. In fact Pinker offers no evidence on this point and mere absence of a theoretical orientation cannot itself be taken as proof of resistance. For another, the lack of a theoretical structure is not peculiar to British social administration. Ignoring some national differences in intellectual orientation, it would seem that a theoretically developed science of social administration is not to be found anywhere, even in countries such as Germany, where social services developed early and *laissez-faire* theories have had little influence. Indeed, if anything, the subject is more academically developed in Britain.[4] Thus the non-theoretical approach may have more to do with the nature of social administration as a social practice than with its British ancestry in the reaction against *laissez-faire* doctrines. One would not be far wrong in suggesting that theorising is almost irrelevant to the main aims of social administration. The frame of reference, the problematic, of the subject itself discourages, if not rules out, conceptual and speculative preoccupation.

In different ways the rationale of social administration – the underlying value premises and aims – has been expressed quite well by Donnison, Warham and Broady among others.[5] Stated simply, the advancement of welfare rather than the accumulation and refinement of a body of tested knowledge is the central concern. Commitment is not so much to interpretation as to changing (or perhaps 'mending' is the better term?) the world. This concern with intervention, with praxis, social administration shares with the Marxist approach. But if Marxism is the science of socialism and revolutionary practice, social administration is the science of reformism, of administrative interventionism and piecemeal social engineering, underpinned by the values of compassion and justice as well as efficiency. Given this concern with amelioration – with the improvement of conditions – social administration is likely to concentrate on practical problems of social policy. Gauging the dimensions of a problem, evaluating past policy, making some implicit or explicit recommendation for future action have been and are likely to be the stock-in-trade of social administration. It follows that the centre of attention must be the national situation – for example, the problems and policies in Britain. As Pinker observes, 'the study of comparative social administration scarcely exists . . . [and] the discipline has remained stubbornly resistant to comparative treatment'.[6] But this is not, as Pinker alleges, because basic and reliable studies of social-policy developments in other countries are lacking. It is rather because given the necessary concern with the details of the social services and policies of one's own country – how effective they are in meeting needs, the nature and dimension of the needs and the like – welfare systems of other countries are necessarily of marginal relevance. Undoubtedly a comparative dimension will be helpful in many ways, not least in countering ethnocentric and insular views of welfare. All the same, it is most unlikely that the central concern of the subject could be anything other than national problems and policies.

Another feature of social administration, related to its practical and interventionist concerns, is its almost exclusive focus on government policies – chiefly the social services. While leading practitioners of the subject have officially recognised the limitations of equating social policy with statutory services, recognised as such, social administration remains firmly wedded to the social services. More than twenty years have passed since Titmuss drew attention to the fact that the social services, fiscal policies and occupational benefits performed similar functions.[7] Titmuss's paper has since become a classic. Yet forms of welfare other than the social services continue a somewhat peripheral and shadowy existence in the context of social administration. Up to a point, this concern with the social services is perfectly valid for undoubtedly they form the core element in modern systems of welfare. On the other hand there is little doubt that the interventionist and reforming concerns of the subject do not encourage the study of non-statutory forms of welfare. The result is that the study of welfare as a whole is inhibited.

A further point that merits attention is the supra-disciplinary character of social administration. As Donnison points out, it is a field of study rather than a discipline [8] (examples of the former are education, welfare, crime; of the latter economics, sociology, psychology). Naturally those concerned with a field are not bound by disciplinary considerations. They may, and normally do, bring the insights and methods of any discipline or of several in combination to bear on the problem in hand. This too militates against, if not rules out, an overt theoretical orientation for the subject matter as a whole.

Given these basic features of social administration it is not surprising that there are no general concepts of welfare or explanations of its development that could be associated with those working within this perspective. And in so far as distinct theoretical (rather than normative) positions can be discerned they are likely to be eclectic – often various mixes of the perspectives we outline later. However, this eclecticism is a necessary feature of any field-orientated (one is tempted to use the term 'applied' but this can be misleading) study. It must also be pointed out that without being overtly concerned with theoretical problems and generalisations, students of social administration have made a valuable contribution (even if somewhat obliquely) to the understanding of society-welfare relationship. Indeed what has been characterised as an atheoretical orientation of social administration, i.e. a factual corrective to grand theories of the economists, can be seen as a perfectly respectable theoretical enterprise. In the language of Karl Popper, the philosopher of scientific method, social administration may be said to have been engaged, albeit implicitly, in the refutation of established theories or conjectures – a perfectly valid scientific method for seeking truth.[9] As Broady points out, what Titmuss and many others have been doing for the area of income distribution and social welfare is not very different from what many sociologists have been doing for social stratification.[10] Both groups of scholars have been testing theses or theories with reference to evidence. The difference of course is that social administration is unable or unwilling to go beyond a critical and refutational stance largely based on data. What it lacks is any explicit theoretical concern. Thus no attempt is made to develop alternative theories and hypotheses and there is little by way of a theoretical (as distinct from normative) debate in the field. This, as we have suggested above, stems largely from the nature of social administration as a social practice. On the other hand it must be remembered that it is only recently that social administration has become established as an academic subject in the universities. And it may well be, as Broady for example claims, that there is already a move towards a 'more theoretically-grounded analysis of social policy'. It is also probable that the critique of Pinker and others may help to develop a 'sociology of welfare' which would be able to address itself to theoretical issues far more easily. However that may be, at present the main features of social administration seem to be the following: first, concern with national policies and problems; second, an interventionist and prescriptive approach; third, focus on statutory welfare; fourth, a field rather than disciplinary orientation; and fifth, empiricism or concern largely with the facts of welfare.

These characteristics put social administration in a class apart from the various perspectives outlined in later chapters. Unlike the latter, social administration is not a theory of welfare. None the less it is the intellectual and ideological framework within which the subject matter of welfare is and has been primarily studied. On these grounds alone it merits further attention.

Social Administration: An Assessment

What are the main strengths and weaknesses of this approach? And what, if any, are its potentialities for developing a more theoretically-based framework for the study of welfare? These and other related questions are best considered in relation to some of the main characteristics of this approach isolated above, namely national focus, interventionism, non-disciplinary or field orientation and empiricism. What are the implications of these for the understanding of welfare as an aspect of society?

(a) National focus Undoubtedly there are good reasons why social administration is largely concerned with the problems and policies of a particular country. But every intellectual strategy has its benefits as well as costs. One of the costs of this approach is to inhibit generalisations about welfare. To quote Pinker again, 'The current lack of adequate comparative analysis in social policy and administration encourages students of social welfare to overemphasise the distinctive nature of social welfare problems in each national context.' [11]

While agreeing with Pinker I am inclined to go further and suggest that this exclusive national focus tends to have a deleterious effect on consciousness about welfare. Let me quote Wedderburn on this. 'In the immediate post-war years the welfare state was generally regarded as an almost exclusively British phenomenon . . . it came as something of a surprise to the insular British to discover at the time of the major debate of her entry into the Common Market that many Western European countries had social security provisions which could provide better benefits than did their British counterparts.' [12] It is arguable that a good deal of complacency about the welfare state in Britain in the 1950s and early 1960s was due to false consciousness of this kind, namely that high levels of taxation and comprehensive social services were exclusively British phenomena. Ideological vested interests – for example those who saw the social services as a child of the post-war Labour Government and as a major instalment of socialism, or again those on the Right who wished to extol national virtues, viz. the peculiar genius of the British people for pragmatism, for compromise, for a commonsensical and practical approach – may have encouraged this view. However that may be, the welfare state tended to be seen as a peculiarly British institution. Happily the social and intellectual climate has changed a good deal since and there is a far greater appreciation of developments outside Britain. None the less the national focus within which the whole social policy debate has largely proceeded tends, unwittingly of course, to present a distorted picture of the significance of the British welfare state. Thus the national health service has rightly been seen as a pioneering British contribution to social policy in the West. What tends to be overlooked, however, is the contribution of other nations and peoples which might put British developments into perspective. How many students of social policy are aware of the lead taken by New Zealand in the development of social services? [13] Thus in the late 1930s, well before Britain emerged from the experience of war with a centralised health service and a far more collectivist social policy, New Zealand had decided to set up a national health service. [14] Perhaps more significantly, the development of social policy on the European continent, notably in Germany, has been almost entirely neglected. The social and political significance of Bismarck's welfare state and later, that of Nazi Germany, has not featured to any great extent on the curriculum of social policy studies in Britain. Against this background, the Marxist allegation that in Britain and the English-speaking world generally state collectivism (including the welfare state) tends to be seen as a kind of socialism becomes more comprehensible. The question of the meaning of the welfare state, of how people in Britain and other countries have perceived changes of this nature, is of course a highly complex issue and simplistic notions of false consciousness can hardly explain why the situation comes to be defined as it is. But there can be little doubt that the study of social welfare within an exclusively national framework has, if not encouraged, at least failed to counteract ethnocentric views about welfare. From this standpoint, broader perspectives such as Marxism or convergence theory which suggest that the development of social services has more to do with capitalism or industrialism than this or that nation, have considerable liberating potential. Ideally what a study of British social policy needs to do is to situate the unique, peculiarly British features within the context of more general developments and unifying themes concerning modern societies. But a framework of study concerned with Britain alone is, naturally, unable to do this.

The problem is not confined to the notion of welfare. In a slightly different form it also arises in connection with explanation of development and change in welfare. If the focus is almost exclusively on British development, generalisations are strictly speaking not possible. On the other hand since social administration is not totally devoid of general ideas about the development of social policy, implicit generalisations tend to be made on the basis of British experience alone. More commonly, perhaps, the British pattern tends to be equated unconsciously with the general pattern. In any case one implication is that some very interesting and insightful studies of society-welfare relationship have remained no more than interpretations of British history. Thus Titmuss's study of the relation between war and social policy [15] has never been examined outside the British context. Consequently we do not know how important war as such has been in promoting collectivist social policies and whether there were some peculiar features associated with the kind of war fought by Britain. In short, the status of war as a factor in social policy development remains somewhat ambiguous. The same could be said of Titmuss's masterly analysis of the development of health care policy in Britain.[16] A major theme of Titmuss's study is the influence of changing medical technology, refracted through the structure of the medical profession, on the organisation of medical care. To put it simply, Titmuss stresses the ways in which social policy has been influenced by medical technology and certain related problems facing the medical profession. This is argued as a corrective to the naive and one-sided view that socialised medicine in Britain has developed out of concern with social justice and the pressure of working-class demands.[17] Once again, however, outside the context of Titmuss's analysis the status of these explanatory variables remains problematic. Since Titmuss is not a technological determinist the presumption must be that the problems posed by changing medical technology could have been solved in a variety of ways. For example in the United States, where presumably similar technological influences were present, the outcome has been very different. This suggests that the decisive influences are socio-political and that, although technology is one of the elements that enters the situation, its influence is mediated by socio-political factors. However, since these British developments have not been compared systematically with other countries, including the United States, we do not know what importance to attach to the various factors involved in the development of health-care systems.[18] Clearly without some reference to at least the class structure, trade unionism and political ideology, the difference in the development of health care in Britain and the United States or other countries cannot be understood. But in the absence of systematic cross-national studies of social policy development, the misleading impression can be conveyed that medical technology has been a major causal factor in the development of the health-care programme. The same argument applies to Titmuss's study of the relation between war and social

policy. The focus on the national situation, then, is likely to encourage ⨉
ad hoc explanations and to inhibit a generalising approach to the
development of welfare.

(b) Interventionism and the problem of values Social administration is
not alone in its interventionist approach to welfare. As we shall see
later, Marxism too involves prescription and intervention, albeit of a
rather total kind. Interventionism, whether of the Marxian or
pragmatic kind, presupposes value judgements. And while the idea of
a value-free social science has rightly been discredited, the academic
study of social issues must be distinguished from the committed approach of a socio-political movement. One of the risks that an interventionist approach such as social administration runs is that a particular value position may be so much taken for granted that its implications are not recognised clearly. True, unlike sociology, social administration has never claimed to be a value-free enterprise. Indeed,
almost by definition, any form of debate on policy, over the choice of
ends and means for instance, cannot be value-free. This much is fairly
evident. It also remains true that the blend of 'fact finding' and 'moral
rhetoric' characteristic of social administration[19] offers little scope for
concealed value judgements. On the other hand if, as Pinker argues,
social administration 'remains relatively free of those ambivalences of
feeling which inhere in the very notion of normative theory'[20] this is
partly because it has not faced up to the problems of values clearly.
For the fact that a discipline makes no claim of scientific detachment,
objectivity and the like is no guarantee that the nature of its value
judgements – direct or indirect – are quite clear to its practitioners and
others. Thus Pinker cites the debate over residual and institutional
models of social policy – central to social administration – as an example that the protagonists come clean with their value judgements.[21]
That this is a debate over values is clear enough. What is not so readily apparent is the fact that in defining and conducting the debate in
terms of the two models, certain other ways of looking at welfare tend
to be ruled out. What is involved here is an implicit value judgement, a
tacit understanding of the limits within which the debate on welfare is
to be carried on. Here the argument of Bachrach and Baratz that
power is not simply about how issues are decided, but also about what
issues are decided, or rather what is excluded from reaching the
decision-making stage, is relevant.[22] Bachrach and Baratz were
concerned with political practice, but the argument applies equally

well to ideological practice. To put it in another form, concepts can
never be presumed innocent. Explicit value stances may conceal more
fundamental value orientations which remain implicit – and therefore
hidden from view. The point can be illustrated with reference to poverty. The problem of poverty has been and remains a central theme in
social reform. Yet the implications of defining a particular situation in
the language of poverty are only recently beginning to be appreciated.
As Westergaard points out 'a good deal of recent research into the distribution of wealth and welfare has been associated with the attempt to
map the contour of poverty. This definition of problems and objectives
carries certain risks. The risks are those in the first instance of identifying, or seeming to identify, poverty as a distinct condition to be
studied, and perhaps remedied, without reference to the larger
organization of economy and society.' [23] He goes on to say that if
attention is focused on various categories of the poor, 'it takes more
than just occasional statement of the point to remember that their conditions are extreme manifestations of the wider class-structured
pattern of inequality in economy and society at large'.[24] Westergaard
puts it rather mildly. In fact a backward glance at the development of
poverty studies in the hands of Booth, Rowntree and others, shows
clearly what this approach involves. Briefly, it means labelling certain
extreme results of social stratification as a social problem and attempting to solve it administratively, that is in a way that does not involve
changes of a more basic kind. In a sense it is a solution at the level of
symptoms rather than causes. It could therefore be argued that to
label the extreme consequences of stratification as poverty, and to
seek a solution through piecemeal social measures, is to accept the
structural inequalities of capitalism. Indirectly, then, it is a decision to
keep the problem within the bounds of capitalism. That this is the case
becomes clear when we consider that the inspirations behind social
policy have been couched in such terms as a 'minimum of civilised existence' (the Webbs), or a modicum of 'social rights' (Marshall). Clearly such policy objectives are quite compatible with and need not dis-
turb the structural inequalities of capitalism. Yet there seems to be
very little awareness of the value implications of this particular approach to welfare.

   To put the problem somewhat differently one might say that social
administration operates with two basic models of social policy –-
residual (conservative) and institutional (liberal/social democratic) –

and almost totally ignores a third model of welfare which might be called 'normative'. This is a view of welfare based on Marxist analysis of the capitalist system and of its eventual supersession by socialism. Briefly, it proposes the institutionalisation of welfare as a central social value, but frankly admits that this cannot be achieved within the confines of capitalism. Why this particular conception of welfare and of social action orientated toward such a goal should be excluded from the study of social administration remains unclear. Yet without the notion of a continuum of social policy ranging from the residual (in ideal-type terms a totally market-based distribution with a poor law type social provision) at one end to the normative (totally need-based distribution summed up by the phrase 'to each according to his needs') at the other it is difficult to make sense of the so-called institutional model. The only logic discernible behind the institutional view is that it represents a mix – a compromise between the residual and normative conceptions. But to ignore the normative view of welfare altogether and to conduct the policy debate in terms of residual versus institutional models is to obscure the real nature of the latter.

A not dissimilar problem raised by the interventionist framework centres on the question of choice. Clearly a policy-orientated approach to welfare – concerned more or less directly with decision-making – presupposes a choice between various alternatives. The problem is that the rhetoric of choice can conceal ambiguities – of reasoning as well as value judgements. In social sciences it is difficult enough to keep a semblance of distinction between the descriptive and prescriptive modes of discourse. But the entanglement can get far worse with perspectives such as Marxism or reformism, with value commitments so evidently involved. This can be illustrated with reference to Titmuss's study *The Gift Relationship*.[25] The book is concerned with the role of altruism – of giving – in modern society. The 'case-study' around which Titmuss builds his argument for the institutionalisation of altruism is the blood transfusion service. On the procurement, distribution and use of blood in medical care – an aspect of social policy about which little is known and information hard to come by – Titmuss succeeds in marshalling a good deal of comparative data including the result of a survey of blood donors in Britain. In many ways the work is vintage Titmuss. A painstaking piece of research into a highly relevant aspect of modern health care, it demonstrates convincingly the all-round superiority of a free and voluntary system of blood donation and use such as exists in Britain. The contrast with the largely commercialised and market-based system in operation in the U.S.A. is telling. In short the book succeeds in making out a strong case for an altruistic (British) rather than ego-istic (American) social policy. But Titmuss's rhetoric of 'choice' goes beyond this. He castigates various determinisms, such as Marxist or technological, for the absence of a morality of choice – a choice that is not already implicit in the nature of economic and social structures.[26] Characteristically Titmuss underlines the point with a quotation from Solzhenitsyn: 'We have to show the world a society in which all relationships, fundamental principles and laws flow directly from moral ethics and from them *alone.*'[27] Social policy, writes Titmuss, is concerned with allowing individuals 'more *freedom of choice* [italics mine] for the expression of altruism'.[28] Indeed one of the theses advanced in the book is that 'modern societies now require more rather than less *freedom of choice* for the expression of altruism in the daily life of all social groups' (italics mine).[29] This insistence on choice, on acting from moral considerations alone is, however, oddly inconsis-tent with the more sociological point made in the book, namely the need for the institutionalisation of altruism. One of the principal arguments of Titmuss is that 'the ways in which society organises and structures its social institution – particularly its health and welfare systems – can encourage or discourage the altruistic in man'.[30] Thus the expanding commercial blood_programmes in the U.S.A., Japan and other countries, writes Titmuss, 'are driving out the voluntary (i.e. altruistic) system' of free donation and use of blood.[31] In short, Titmuss is forced to acknowledge that in the absence of in-stitutionalisation, altruistic action is likely to give way to egoistic. But this institutionalised morality – an institutional constraint which in-duces individuals to act in a certain way – is a far cry from the rhetoric of a moral choice unconnected with social and economic structure. In effect, Titmuss's position is far closer to the sociological determinism of a Durkheim or even a Marx than his rhetoric would suggest.

The framework of choice and intervention raises another question that is easily overlooked. What are the limits, the structural con-straints, within which choice is exercised? In principle of course a free and democratic society can opt for anything that is supported by the majority. But in fact we know that value conflicts and decision-making take place within a tacit consensus which rules out various utopian and impractical approaches. Indeed social administrators are not unaware of such structural constraints. Thus Donnison writes, 'Since they (the social services) are so deeply embedded in society, it follows that they cannot grow in a stable, liberal democracy without the consent of the major interests – political, industrial, religious or administrative – that hold power in such a society.' [32] However, since such insights are more in the nature of 'asides' rather than a part of the social administrator's script, the limits within which choice is normally exercised can be too readily forgotten. This encourages a stance of bureaucratic or reformist existentialism which ignores the hard realities of structure. Finally, an interventionist or policy framework, inclined to overlook the constraints of the social structure, can too readily assume that choices once made can be translated into more or less enduring social institutions. In short, the insistence on freedom of choice and action may blind one to the problem of successful institutionalisation of values that are not the dominant ones in a particular social system. Behind much of Titmuss's polemics in *The Gift Relationship* (and in other works) is the idea of the corrosive influence of market capitalism which threatens to erode the values and institutions of the welfare state. But the framework of choice does not lend itself easily to an examination of the relevant structural constraints – structural relations which might throw light on the preconditions for the realisation of the idea of welfare as well as the ways in which 'good' choices may be turned into something quite different through the workings of dominant values and institutions. One may, however, choose to disregard such structural 'determinism'. This is probably implied in Titmuss's rejection of 'both the notion of historical inevitability in the making of social policy and the fetish of the final solution'.[33] One implication of this seems to be the decision to conduct the struggle for welfare within the framework of capitalist democracy. In short, liberal capitalism is taken for granted as the framework within which the see-sawing battle between capitalistic and welfare-orientated values is to be waged perpetually.

(c) Empiricism We turn next to social administration's empirical orientation – its concentration on 'facts' rather than theories and interpretations of welfare. Given the concern with reform and intervention, it is natural that quantification of the dimensions of a problem remains central to the subject. It is not only that policy research, in a narrow

sense, demands a focus on data. The tradition of piecemeal reformism within a consensual framework also encourages the strategy of exposure and publicity, of the dramatic revelation of facts in order to shock public opinion out of complacency. Indeed we would suggest that *pace* Pinker it is not so much opposition to *laissez-faire* economic theories or to the Poor Law Report of 1834 that is responsible for the empirical orientation of social administration. It is rather its concern with amelioration within a framework of social and moral consensus. Appeal to facts has a ring of political neutrality and impartiality that ideological positions lack. It allows the case for social reform to be presented as a matter of 'common sense', 'humanity' and 'justice' rather than a question of doctrine. Indeed given the objectives of the reformers, the strategy of presenting facts and appealing to a range of diffuse values and concerns – fairness, compassion, efficiency – seems to have served the cause well. At any rate the cause of social welfare has attracted and continues to attract a wide range of public opinion of all political shades. That it has also meant abstracting out a set of problems from more basic structural concerns and relationships remains true. Given the limited objectives of social reform, however, this may be an advantage. *Ad hoc* 'problems' which, given goodwill and compassion, can be solved largely through administrative techniques (social insurance as a solution of poverty, for example) do not question, let alone attack, the legitimacy of the dominant values and institutions. A wide spectrum of public opinion can therefore be enlisted in support of the cause. The Webbs' tactic of 'permeation' epitomises such a factual, non-partisan approach. In short, social administration's grounding in facts cannot simply be seen as a continuing reaction to nineteenth-century economic theories. The empirical approach seems far more integral to social administration as a social activity.

Theoretically-inclined students of social welfare naturally find this empiricism frustrating (Pinker for example) while many sociologists rate this approach as no more than 'social book-keeping' (Rex). There is, however, a far more important side to concern with facts which needs emphasising. It is that certain kinds of facts can have far-reaching social implications. The ruling powers of any society, including those in the West, do not take kindly to awkward facts about that society being revealed. Totalitarian regimes rely on the systematic suppression of information as a method of political control. This is not the case in the West. None the less, despite the explosion of information and the unprecedented growth in communications of all kinds, significant facts, especially those concerning the structure of power and privilege, are hard to come by. In any case the complexities of the modern industrial society make it harder rather than easier to establish the contours and the credentials of data relevant to a particular issue, for example stratification. Viewed in this light, the contribution of social administration – at any rate the contribution of those like Titmuss who interpret their academic brief widely – has been seminal. The point at issue is not simply the knowledge-base necessary for informed social criticism. It is also a question of the evidence-base necessary for social theorising (unless, that is, one believes in a 'fact-free' sociology). Not surprisingly the Kafkaesque maze of complexity of stratification in advanced capitalist society revealed in Titmuss's works contrasts oddly with the preoccupation of a good deal of academic sociology with such banalities as the functionalist theory of stratification. In short, the lack of theoretical orientation should not be × allowed to obscure the strengths of the 'empirical' tradition. It is not without significance that both Marxism (or at least some of its national variants) and social administration show a far greater concern with social facts than does for instance 'professional' sociology. For unlike the latter, both Marxism and social administration entail socially committed standpoints. Neither believes in the ivory tower quest for 'objective' social knowledge. Knowledge and theorising is valued not so much for its own sake but as an aid to understanding, as a leverage for changing the world.

(d) Multi-disciplinary approach Finally, we come to the method of study – the basic academic orientation of social administration. Very simply the question is that given its supra-disciplinary or 'field' orientation what are the prospects for the development of a conceptually rigorous and systematic approach? Let us begin by noting that social administrators are by no means in agreement about the nature of the subject. Donnison, for example, sees it simply as a 'field' – a problem area to which scholars with a variety of disciplinary backgrounds and skills contribute. The 'distinctive feature of social administration', writes Donnison, 'is neither its body of knowledge (for most of this could be incorporated in other disciplines), nor its theoretical structure (for it has very little), and it is not concerned with methodology for its own sake'.[34] Titmuss on the other hand believes that

as a subject, social administration has begun to develop a body of knowledge and a related set of concepts and principles. It is in the process of knowledge-building which is one of the attributes of science. In doing so, it has borrowed heavily from different disciplines in the social sciences and now faces the task of refining, extending and adapting insights, perspectives and methods so as to further our understanding of the roles and functions of social services in contemporary society.[35]

Clearly, Titmuss sees social administration as rather more than a field in the Donnison sense. He seems to believe that it is in the course of emerging as a subject in its own right, drawing on various basic disciplines but graduating on to a stage where it becomes, so to speak, a 'synthetic discipline'. However, the difference between these two views of social administration may be more apparent than real. For it is likely that it is a matter of description in the one case (Donnison) and prescription or anticipation in the other (Titmuss).

However this may be, what direction social administration as an academic enterprise will take in future must remain a matter of speculation. It is reasonable to suggest, however, that given its comparatively recent establishment as a subject in higher education it will tend to become more theoretical and will draw increasingly on sociology as its theory-base. But as Joyce Warham argues,[36] in my view perceptively and convincingly, this should not be taken to mean that social administration will or ought to become 'sociology of welfare' — a specialism within the discipline of sociology. Warham quite rightly insists on the importance of the distinction and believes a complementary relation between the two to be the most fruitful. But if social administration is to remain distinctive and yet become more academic and theoretical, is there a particular form, a direction, in which it might develop? Could criminology as an academic subject be relevant as a model? Curiously enough Warham does mention criminology but merely to suggest that sociology of welfare might come to play a part in relation to social administration similar to criminology.[37] In fact criminology, in many ways, seems to offer a very appropriate model of a 'synthetic discipline' for social administration. It shows quite clearly that the study of a 'field' need not be *ad hoc* and atheoretical, that social relevance and utility are not incompatible with intellectual stimulus and excitement and finally that it is possible to fashion an academic identity that is genuinely supra-disciplinary and synthetic. This is not to deny that there are important differences between criminology and social administration. Moreover, in bracketing them together I do not for a moment wish to suggest that the latter is concerned with social pathology. As for 'sociology of welfare', it could stand in relation to social administration where 'sociology of deviance' stands in relation to criminology. For the one is an area specialism within sociology (welfare/deviance) whereas the other is a field study focused on a specific problem (crime/social needs) and on the relevant social institutions and organisation. The former seeks to develop the discipline in relation to a particular aspect of society. The latter draws on a range of contributory skills and disciplines to focus on a particular set of issues and problems.

To conclude: as an approach to the study of welfare, social administration presents a range of strengths. Among these are social relevance, practicality, commitment to humanitarian values, concern with society and change in a direct and immediate sense. However the characteristic features of social administration – the source of its strength – also preclude a generalising and theoretical approach focused on society-welfare relationship. Indeed it can hardly be otherwise with what is essentially an 'applied' social science. This is not to deny its importance, and valuable contribution, to the study and practice of welfare. It is rather that for an adequate theoretical view of welfare we must turn to other approaches.

Chapter 2

Welfare as Citizenship

Unlike social administration the citizenship view offers a descriptive (rather than prescriptive) and generalising perspective on welfare, albeit one that is confined to state welfare and its development in Western democratic societies. In a now-famous essay, published shortly after the war, Marshall put forward the view of the social services as a component of citizenship rights in the modern democratic state.[1] To be precise, however, Marshall's work is concerned with Britain and makes no claim for more general validity. Can its basic argument be generalised for Western societies as a whole? Marshall's discussion is limited to Britain, but he writes as a sociologist[2] rather than as a social historian concerned solely with British developments. His analysis seems to be about welfare in a generic sense even if the setting is British. Thus as a sociological explanation his work may be seen as having some general validity for societies similar to Britain. In any case the concept of citizenship rights has had a wide currency as a valid interpretation of certain social and political developments in modern nation-states. Sociologists of varying theoretical persuasion, for example Parsons, Bendix and Lenski, have found Marshall's concept useful.[3] The citizenship view of welfare can therefore be seen as valid for at least Western industrial countries, whose political and economic structure is broadly similar to that of Britain.

Social Rights and their Development

Marshall's analysis is chiefly concerned with the development of citizenship rights and its impact on social inequality. These rights, according to Marshall, consist of three different elements – civil, political and social. The first refers broadly to guarantees of individual liberty and equality before the law; the second to political enfranchisement – the right to vote and to seek political office; the third, a good deal less specific than the other two, comprises a 'modicum of economic welfare and security' and the 'right to share to the full in the social heritage and life of a civilized being according to the standards prevailing in the society'. The first of these rights inheres basically in the legal institutions, the second in the political institutions and the third in the social services. Marshall traces the development of these rights in England in some detail down to the mid-twentieth century. The major development of each is located within a particular period: civil rights in the eighteenth century, political rights in the nineteenth century and social rights in the twentieth century.

Implicit in Marshall's historical analysis is the idea of change from a pre-industrial to an industrial society – from a communally-based social order (*Gemeinschaft*) to one that is based on more formal and rational relationships (*Gesellschaft*).[5] But this change is examined in the context of Britain, as an evolutionary development of a particular society. All three constituent rights of citizenship have roots going far back into English history. Essentially, their development involves a widening of scope, for example to include the whole population, and in this sense also their democratisation and redefinition in the context of modern society. Thus political rights, initially restricted to the aristocracy were extended first to the middle classes, thence to the working classes and finally to women. Similarly social rights, in the form of the Poor Law, were at first restricted to the needy (further restricted to the destitute in the nineteenth century); as social services they were later extended to the working classes and eventually to the whole population.

The rights of citizenship are essentially norms that define the membership of a large-scale, democratic, industrial community. In other words, these rights have a direct bearing on social solidarity in modern societies. According to Marshall, modern societies require a bond different in kind from the traditional forms of solidarity based on 'ascribed' status typical of the pre-industrial societies. Solidarity in modern conditions entails 'a direct sense of community membership based on loyalty of free men endowed with rights and protected by a common law. Its growth is stimulated both by the struggle to win these rights and their enjoyment when won.'[6] Citizenship, then, is a form of equality of status as a member of the 'societal community' = the modern nation-state. Civil, political and social rights together form the basis for the full membership of a modern community. The relation between the three remains somewhat unclear in Marshall's work. But civil and, especially, political rights help the development of social rights which in turn enable the full and proper exercise of the other two. A minimum of education and of income, health and housing is a necessary condition for the full exercise of civil and political rights. Social rights, so to speak, round off the other two; they contribute both to the sentiment of solidarity – the sense of belonging to a community – as well as to effective participation as a member of the community.

In examining the relation between social rights and social stratification Marshall returns to the theme of community. The starting point of his analysis here is the paradox that the growth of citizenship – which has to do with equality – has coincided with the development of capitalism, a system of inequality. However, the paradox is more apparent than real for, as Marshall observed, citizenship has to do with equality of status as a member of a community and not with equality in any other sense. Thus equal status as a citizen is quite compatible with inequality in other respects, for example material rewards, resulting from the operations of the market and other structures of capitalism.[7] Indeed, as Wedderburn has pointed out, Marshall was one of the earliest among sociologists to recognise that the welfare state is not, primarily, an egalitarian measure.[8] He wrote: 'the extension of the social services is not primarily a means of equalizing incomes. In some cases it may, in others it may not. The question is relatively unimportant; it belongs to a different department of social policy.'[9] Neither the primary objectives nor the consequences of state welfare are egalitarian in the sense of reducing class inequality. As Marshall pointed out, with the social services the redistribution of incomes and life-chances tends to be mainly horizontal (within classes) rather than vertical (between classes). Far from reducing class inequality, citizenship creates an equality of conditions in certain respects in order that a structure of social inequality may be built all the more securely. It provides 'the foundation of equality on which the structure of inequality could be built'.[10] In this sense the welfare state makes inequality more acceptable and legitimate.

Marshall, however, recognised some tension between the equality of citizenship and the inequalities of capitalism. And referring specifically to post-war Britain he thought that the 'enrichment' of the status of citizenship was making 'the preservation of economic inequalities' more difficult.[11] From the vantage of the 1970s, Marshall's main contribution appears to have been to show that social rights, like civil and political rights, are quite compatible with capitalism and its class structure. Here Marshall stands closer to the Marxists than to social-democrats, many of whom see (or have seen) the welfare state as a socialist and egalitarian measure. However, as we shall see later, with its emphasis on community and solidarity, the citizenship view of welfare is closer to the functionalist approach. It is no mere coincidence that Talcott Parsons, the high priest of modern functionalism, should employ Marshall's ideas to depict the growth and consolidation of the 'nation as societal community' in modern times.[12]

The affinity with functionalism is also evident in Marshall's view of the *development* of citizenship rights. Thus group conflict, concerning values and interests, finds no place in his account of the growth of citizenship which is presented as an evolutionary process. True, conflict makes its appearance from time to time but only as conflict between the various 'rights'. On the whole the process of development is seen as linear and incremental. Now this fits the case of civil and political rights quite well but not that of social rights. For unlike the other two, which show a more or less steady, linear progression (from about the eighteenth and the early nineteenth centuries respectively), social rights in England have had a chequered career. Thus the Speenhamland system of poor relief (early nineteenth century) represents a sort of high water mark in the recognition of social rights within a pre-modern framework of welfare. But with the deterrent poor law policy of 1834, which was to last through the best part of the nineteenth century, social rights suffered a sharp setback. In Marshall's words they 'sank to vanishing point'.[13] Their 'revival began with the development of public elementary education, but it was not until the twentieth century that they attained to equal partnership with the other two elements of citizenship'.[14] Why social rights should have had these ups and downs is not explained. Or rather the explanation offered is circular – in terms of the individual history of each of the rights. In pre-modern (feudal) England all three rights were fused together in the matrix of custom and tradition. But with the passing of the old order they parted company and 'it became possible for each to go its separate way, travelling at its own speed under the direction of its own peculiar principles'.[15] But these 'peculiar principles' are nowhere elaborated and what we are offered is a narrative, a historical sketch, of the separate development of each of the rights. Marshall's account reads essentially like the story of the gradual and inevitable realisation of a certain concept of citizenship inherent in the nature and development of English society. Despite some sociological under-pinning, it is strongly reminiscent of Dicey's 'explanation' of the growth of social legislation in England.[16] For Dicey the changing currents of public opinion decided whether individualism or collec-tivism held sway. For Marshall the changing conception of rights won the day.

Citizenship: An Assessment

How adequate is the citizenship view as a theory of welfare? We shall examine the question under three main headings: (a) the concept of welfare; (b) the account of the development of welfare; and (c) im-plications for policy.

(a) The concept of welfare How adequate is social rights as a concept of welfare? To begin with, let us note some of its limitations. First, since it refers to statutory welfare alone it cannot encompass other ways of meeting needs, for example occupational benefits, voluntary and charitable welfare. Despite its focus on the most important com-ponent of welfare in modern society, it fails to provide a framework for an analysis of different types of welfare, their relationship with one another and with the social structure. It could of course be argued that these various forms of welfare stem from different social and economic principles and cannot be examined within the same concep-tual framework. How valid is this argument? Admittedly state welfare differs in important ways from the others. But as we pointed out

earlier (p. 6) Titmuss has shown quite convincingly how misleading it can be to examine the so-called 'social services' in isolation from other ways of meeting needs, notably occupational benefits and fiscal measures. These and other forms of welfare have a good deal in common and in some ways can be seen as alternative methods of meeting needs. For a proper understanding of welfare, then, it is necessary to consider the various need-meeting patterns and their inter-relationship together. From this viewpoint, social rights is a rather limiting concept. Second, its scope seems limited to Western democracies. Clearly state welfare in socialist countries, for example the U.S.S.R., can hardly be understood in terms of citizenship. For if these countries have gone a long way towards providing 'social rights' they have been most reluctant to grant civil and political rights of the kind that exist in the West. In short, the social services in socialist countries cannot be seen as a set of rights which are part and parcel, let alone a consequence, of the development of citizenship. But how valid is the concept in relation to Western societies?

Social services, according to this interpretation, are essentially the material expression of a set of rights of citizenship – similar to civil and political rights. Seen in this way social rights appear as a set of self-evident principles inherent in the notion of modern citizenship which receive due recognition in the post-war British welfare state. Yet as Marshall's own analysis shows, over the last two centuries the definition (and not merely the definition) of these rights has undergone a series of changes.[17] This suggests that the post-war welfare state may have been no more than a contingent phenomenon, a result of the conjunction of social forces prevalent in Britain around the Second World War.[18] In Marshall's account, however, the welfare state acquires a *necessary* character. There is a suggestion of inevitability in the way the third element in citizenship, namely social rights, eventually develops to complement the other two. A close scrutiny of Marshall's own definition, however, leaves us in little doubt about the problematic and contingent nature of these rights. Social rights, according to Marshall, consist of 'the whole range from the right to a modicum of economic welfare and security to the right to share to the full in the social heritage and to live the life of a civilized being according to the standards prevailing in the society.'[19] But what is a 'modicum' of economic welfare and security? And what, precisely, does 'the right to share to the full in the social heritage' mean? Or for that matter 'the life of a civilized being according to the standards prevailing in the society'? Whose standards? Who is to decide what these standards are to be? The point need not be laboured. It is quite clear that the nature and content of social rights are neither self-evident nor given. Yet the whole question of the *level* of social provision which is the crux of the matter and which is so obviously bound up with group interests, values and beliefs and the distribution of power in society is glossed over in Marshall's *ad hoc* and *a priori* notion of citizenship. In short 'social rights' as such do not tell us what their content at any time in a particular society would be. For example, it could be argued that public elementary education of the kind provided in England towards the close of the nineteenth century meets the requirements of citizenship quite well and that the educational changes of this century have gone far beyond the basic rights of citizens to receive a modicum of education. The provision of 'optimal' medical care under the National Health Service has a similar implication. In short, what 'social rights' the population of a modern democratic state will enjoy cannot be determined in advance by some *a priori* notion of citizenship rights.

This becomes quite clear when one looks at countries other than Britain. Let us take for example the United States, an industrial society politically and culturally similar to Britain. In the United States, civil and political rights (at least for the white male population) became established quite early.[20] Social rights on the other hand, with the notable exception of education, have been extremely slow to develop.[21] Indeed it could be said that the dominant ideology in the United States does not recognise social rights as an essential ingredient of citizenship. Germany, likewise, shows a very different relation between social rights and the other two ingredients of citizenship. Bismarck readily conceded social rights to German workers in order to deny full political and civil rights; 'social rights' were a means to contain the development of citizenship in other respects.[22] These examples suggest quite strongly that even within Western societies the relation between the social services on the one hand and civil and political rights on the other, is a complex one and that the notion of citizenship may not be very helpful in explaining the nature and extent of state intervention in welfare.

Another way of looking at the problem is to recognise that logically social rights do not belong to the same category of norms as civil and political rights. In Western democratic societies, equality before the law and adult franchise form the substance of civil and political rights respectively. Social rights, on the other hand, do not have this discrete, finite character. Which particular services will be incorporated into social rights – that is, distributed according to 'non-market' criteria – and what will be the level of benefits are questions that cannot be settled in the same discrete once-and-for-all manner as in the case of the other two rights. In Western democracies the nature of civil and political rights is not normally a matter of controversy, of policy differences between the parties for example. What controversy there is (for example in the United States with regard to the blacks and in many other countries with regard to women) usually turns on the question of implementation rather than on the nature of the rights themselves. By contrast social policy, in Britain and elsewhere, constitutes the very stuff and substance of domestic political controversy. In part this is because social rights are concerned with the distribution of the social product whereas civil and political rights are not, at least not directly. Rather they set the institutional framework within which the conflict over distribution – of which the conflict about 'social rights' is a part – takes place. We might say that civil and political rights set the rules of the game: social rights represent the outcome of the game. They are not regulative norms of the same kind as the other two rights. It might be more appropriate to describe the social services as a temporary institutionalisation of a given pattern of resource distribution. Civil and political rights could hardly be described in this way. To subsume social rights under the notion of citizenship rights is to ignore this important distinction.

(b) The Development of Welfare It is because of this basic difference that the analysis is unable to explain the changing character of social rights. What is Marshall's explanation of the fact that they had reached almost 'vanishing point' during a part of the nineteenth century in Britain? It is simply that civil and social rights were in conflict and that the former won the day.[23] But why were they in conflict and what enabled civil rights to triumph over its companion? What social forces stood behind the civil rights – of the freedom of contract – that were so effective in crushing social rights? This is nowhere explained though we are told later that 'civil rights were indispensable to a competitive market economy'.[24] Apparently by giving each man the power to engage as an individual in the economic struggle they 'made it

possible to deny him social protection on the ground that he was equipped with the means to protect himself'.[25] And again, 'civil rights were in origin intensely individual and that is why they harmonised with the individualistic phase of capitalism'.[26] If the sudden demise of social rights in the early nineteenth century receives no satisfactory explanation, their later resurgence appears equally arbitrary. 'Their revival began with the development of public elementary education, but it was not until the twentieth century that they attained to equal partnership with the other two elements in citizenship.'[27] Marshall refers to the extension of political rights in the late nineteenth and early twentieth century, but only in passing. True, at one point he writes that 'the normal method of establishing social rights is by the exercise of political power'.[28] But this important relationship is not used to explain the collapse of social rights in the nineteenth century. Nor is it developed as an explanation of their advancement in the twentieth century.

In general Marshall's account of the development of social rights is in a line with his notion of citizenship rights as inherent in the nature of modern society. The framework of explanation is evolutionary and despite the notion of some conflict between the rights, in general they are seen as complementary. Civil and political rights prepare the ground for the eventual triumph of social rights. What is almost totally missing in Marshall's account is the attempt to relate these rights to changes in social structure. The structural background is sketched in here and there but only in passing. The changing nature of social classes, of ideologies and beliefs, of the shifting balance of power between different social groups and the relevance of all these for the development of the rights is virtually left out of analysis. So is the influence of industrialisation. Moreover, as we have mentioned already social conflict hardly finds a place in Marshall's evolutionary model of social development.

To sum up: first, Marshall's concept of social rights is limited to the social services and leaves out of account other forms of welfare. Second, Marshall's work, largely concerned with the development of the welfare state in England, at best offers a framework for (the examination of) similar developments in Western industrial societies. Linked as it is to civil and political rights, it is not easily applicable to communist countries. In any case the attempt to link social services with the idea of citizenship runs into difficulty. Third, the holistic and evolutionary approach to social change, which ignores the effect of group action and conflict, fails to provide an explanation for the changing nature of the social rights at different periods of English history and, by the same token, between different countries. In brief, the citizenship view of welfare falls far short of a sociologically adequate framework for understanding the nature and development of welfare in modern industrial societies. To say this, however, is not to deny Marshall's pioneering contribution to the exploration of the society-welfare relationship. With the benefit of hindsight we can see the limitations and weaknesses of Marshall's interpretation as well as its strengths.

We have dwelt at length on the limitations of Marshall's work and it seems appropriate to end this section emphasising two of the more positive aspects of his contribution. At a time of great intellectual uncertainty, if not confusion, about the nature of changes that capitalism had undergone, and in particular about the levelling effect of the welfare state, Marshall had the analytical insight to suggest that the idea of a basic minimum of social provision (even if it was sometimes tending towards an 'optimum') was quite compatible with a social organisation based on competition and inequality. Of equal importance was the emphasis Marshall placed on the part that social services can play in creating and maintaining solidarity in conditions of modern society. Marshall's analysis is thus relevant to the problems which in different ways Marx, Spencer and Durkheim had considered.[29] The idea of citizenship can be seen as a bridge between Spencer's affirmation of the contractual basis of solidarity and Durkheim's insistence on the altruistic and collectivist bond as an essential component of social cohesion in modern times. The notion of citizenship comes to terms with the fact that history has overtaken the analyses and prescriptions of both these thinkers. If Spencerian individualism has proved untenable, the solution has not been sought in Durkheimian corporatism.[30] Moreover an attempt has been made to come to terms with the problem of social justice (which Durkheim realised was a precondition of social cohesion but for which he offered no solution) through the institutionalisation of social rights.

(c) Implications for Policy From the viewpoint of policy the main significance of citizenship seems to be that it offers a rationale for an 'institutional' form of social provision in opposition to the earlier *laissez-faire* or 'residual' form. In capitalist society some form of justification is needed for universal, comprehensive, 'as of right' social

services. Citizenship provides such a justification. The social
philosophy underlying the Beveridge Report, for example, is couched
in these terms. It should be noted however that in Britain and other
English-speaking countries, with their pragmatic, empirical approach
to social issues, there has been little need to theorise about social
reform in such abstract terms as citizenship.

All the same, academic debates about social policy do raise the
question of the relevance of the concept. Parker, for example, writes of
its 'attractiveness . . . as a basis for ordering of social relations and the
distribution of public services'.[31] Pinker too sees the values of
citizenship as providing the basic underpinning for Britain's social
services.[32] Part of the appeal of citizenship is, no doubt, that it offers a
neat and in many ways an apolitical conception of the social services.
Its justification for a limited but useful and honourable place for the
social services forms a basis for consensus among people of 'reason
and goodwill' about the role of the welfare state in capitalist society.
Unfortunately, as recent discussions show, the problems involved in
trying to base social policy on citizenship are considerable. The main
problem is the incompatibility of the idea of citizenship as a basis
of resource distribution with the dominant values and beliefs of
capitalism. As Parker puts it, in capitalist society 'Independence,
wealth and the ability to buy services of all kinds are highly regarded,
but a belief in the idea of citizenship would require their opposites to
be similarly approved.'[33] Pinker finds a good deal of ambivalence
surrounding the notion of citizenship in mixed economies such as Britain. In opposition to citizenship and the collectivist values underlying
the social services 'the ideology of self-help and individualism receives
powerful support from the continuing dominance of market values in
our lives'.[34]

In short, the discussion of citizenship in the context of policy echoes
and confirms our earlier critique of the concept. The idea of social
rights itself is useful but the kind of goods and services and the level of
provision that would constitute such rights cannot be decided *a priori*.
Conflicting values and interests lie behind conceptions of social policy
and the idea of citizenship as such cannot extricate us from these
difficulties. Perhaps it ought to be recognised that in some ways we
have moved beyond the stage of social policy development where the
idea of citizenship as such could be a useful guide to policy. For its
main relevance is in legitimating the principle of universal, comprehen-

sive, 'as of right' social services. It therefore seems to have more relevance in the struggle against a residual policy, for example in the United States and Japan rather than in Western Europe generally where the principle of an institutional social policy has become widely accepted. This is not to deny that the idea of social rights – of entitlement to a service without any loss of status – retains its importance in the struggle against 'stigma'. It has to be recognised, moreover, that the dominant values and institutions of capitalism are on the whole quite inimical to the values underlying the social services. In this sense stigma is likely to remain a problem and the battle against residualism has to be waged perpetually. But then it may be better to recognise that social rights can never quite take root in capitalist society in the same way as civil and political rights because the former do not 'belong' to a capitalist social order in the same way as the other two. In short, citizenship may be less helpful a concept for thinking about major issues of social policy though it may still be useful in the struggle against a residual social policy.

However the idea of citizenship is sometimes used in another sense. Here the reference is not to social rights as a basis of social policy but to the exercise of citizenship – in its civil, political and social aspects. In brief, the problem concerns the gap between formal entitlement or the existence of rights and their actual utilisation or enjoyment; between formal equality of status as citizen and the substantive inequality resulting from the facts of stratification. As is well known, one of the main problems with universal social services is that they are often best utilised by those who need them least. Thus how to ensure proper utilisation of services by the poor, how to ensure something like equality of treatment of clients irrespective of education, income, race and the like remains a serious problem. Once again the notion of citizenship is valuable in emphasising the ideal of equality of status and thus indirectly questioning the legitimacy of inegalitarian social relationships of a stratified society. In the optimistic post-war days Marshall believed that the preservation of inequality 'has been made more difficult by the enrichment of the status of citizenship'.[35] With hindsight we can now see which of the two has proved the stronger. The question now seems less how far citizenship can act as the thin end of the wedge of equality and far more whether the ideal of social services free from stigma and class bias can ever be realised.[36]

There are of course many other contexts of social policy, for exam-

Chapter 3

Convergence Theory or Technological Determinism: Welfare System as a Product of Industrialism

[handwritten marginalia: "Citizenship = politics / Convergence = economics" with bracket "necessary to → Combine. Not utter."]

If the citizenship view stresses the role of politics in the development of welfare in modern society, convergence theory emphasises the role of industrialisation in shaping the institutions of welfare. The emphasis on industrialism rather than Western political values and institutions (citizenship) enables this theory to take a wider view of welfare. Unlike citizenship, its perspective is neither limited to social services nor to Western industrial countries alone. In insisting that the decisive fact about modern societies is not their political affiliation as such – in Galbraith's phrase 'ideological billing' – but their industrial character, the theory finds identical structural patterns and influences in both capitalist and socialist society.

The basic theoretical premises of convergence theory are functionalist in nature, but whereas functionalism, as we shall see later, is concerned with the prerequisites of the functioning and integration of social systems in a general way, convergence theory is more specific. It takes industrial and economic development to be the central task of modern societies and believes that it is around this core requirement that the social structure is functionally integrated. In other words, the theory tries to explain the nature and development of the social institutions of industrial societies in terms of the 'pull' (requirements or functional necessities) and the 'push' (consequences) of an industrial technology and economy. Hence, the key determinant of the social structure of advanced industrial society, the theory argues, is neither ideology, nor class conflict, nor again culture, but technology. In the long run, argues the convergence theorist, the range of problems as well as their likely solutions in these societies is heavily conditioned by the consequences and requirements of industrial technology. As Galbraith puts it succinctly, if dogmatically: 'Given the decision to have modern industry, much of what happens is inevitable and the same.'[2]

Industrial Society and Social Welfare

But how does industrialisation influence welfare? Here much of what the theory has to say (or rather suggest, since welfare systems have not been discussed systematically or in any detail in the literature) is common currency in the form of textbook interpretations of social welfare.[3] Let us however sketch in the broad outlines. Industrialisation transforms the nature of the labour force: the 'self-employed' – the farmers, craftsmen and the like – are replaced by workers 'employed' for a wage. Regular income from employment comes to be the main source of livelihood for an increasing proportion of the work force. Industrial employment also imposes a clear-cut distinction between those at work and those out of work. As a result, unemployment, sickness, work injury, old age and the like can bring about a sudden interruption in earnings, and the problem of protection against such contingencies becomes acute. Through urbanisation, industrial development also gives rise to problems of public health, housing and control of the urban environment. Industrial society also requires an educated work force and citizenry. Educating the masses thus becomes a key imperative. Alongside these changes, geographical and occupational mobility increases and the traditional agencies of support – the extended family and the local community – weaken. Thus the stage is set for the development of a host of formally organised patterns – friendly society benefits, charitable assistance, enterprise and state programmes, for example – to meet a variety of emergent needs. In short, industrialisation creates the preconditions for a substantial growth of specialised or 'structurally differentiated' agencies of welfare. But to what extent such agencies would develop and which type will predominate depends, initially at any rate, on factors other than industrialisation *per se*. A major influence on the social structure at the early stages of development is the nature of the industrialising elite. The social group, the elite or social class, leading the process of industrialisation moulds the social structure largely according to its own ideology and interests. Kerr and his colleagues, leading proponents of convergence, distinguish five types of industrialising elites.[4] Three of these – the middle classes, the traditional or dynastic groups and the communists – are especially relevant to the social structure of present day industrial societies. What is the attitude of each of these elites towards welfare?

The middle class believes in the freedom of the market place. It aims at maximising the role of the market in the distribution of rewards and resources and at minimising state intervention. Middle-class values stress individual responsibility and initiative in meeting needs. Paternalism – of the state but also of the employer – is frowned upon. Freedom and self-reliance are encouraged. The regime favours a relatively independent worker, self-reliant economically and politically. Not the bonds of status but those of contract between 'free' men typifies the basic model of social relationship outside the family. Translating these generalities into patterns of welfare, we might say that the middle-class society is likely to develop a 'residual' system of welfare. In the early stages of industrialisation neither state nor enterprise welfare is favoured. Instead, friendly societies, voluntary organisations, charities and market responses to the various problems and needs are encouraged.[5]

By contrast, where industrialisation is led by dynastic or traditional groups, in Germany and Japan for example, social policy tends to be paternalistic. The state and the enterprise accepts responsibility for the workers' welfare far more readily and in turn expects the worker to be loyal. The 'market' and contractual relationship is subordinated to a 'traditional' framework of duties and obligations. Compared to middle-class societies, then, the dynastic societies are far more collectivist. The result is that something like an 'institutional' pattern of welfare – that is, one where the state accepts a measure of responsibility for the workers' needs – begins to be established fairly early in the course of industrial development.[6]

Where communists lead the industrial revolution, the role of the

state is all-encompassing. The communists are out-and-out collec-
tivists and at least in principle, also egalitarians. Hence the family, the
market, individual freedom and responsibility – in short, the basic
values and institutions typical of the middle classes – occupy a lowly
place in the hierarchy of the communist social order. The individual is
subordinated to the collective, and the state acting in the name of the
collective assumes full responsibility for meeting needs. Communist
social policy, at least in principle, is the very opposite of *laissez-faire*.
The state becomes the natural provider of needs, and social services –
catering for a wide range of needs and encompassing the entire population – the 'norm'. In the emphasis on meeting needs through collective social provision and with the virtual state monopoly in this respect
the communist societies go far beyond the 'institutional' approach. In
contrast with the other two forms of welfare, the communist pattern
may thus be described as 'normative'. The distribution of resources on
the basis of need and in the form of state social services is considered
normal, a part of the dominant value system of society.[7]

But these different policies and the resulting patterns of welfare
refer to the early phases of industrialisation. What convergence theory
asserts, above all, is that as societies become more advanced
industrially there is a progressive narrowing of differences. The 'logic'
of industrialism constrains advanced industrial societies towards a
common institutional pattern. But what is the nature of this institutional pattern? The convergence theorist answers this question in
terms of a model, an 'ideal type' of advanced industrial society based
on the functional relation between the industrial economy and the
social structure. The logic of industrialism is the inherent tendency of
existing industrial societies to approximate this ideal. Naturally the
ideal cannot be specified in detail but its basic feature has been
characterised as that of 'pluralistic industrialism'.[8] Essentially, this is
a 'mixed' system – one that lies somewhere between the extremes of
total state control ('monism') and unremitting *laissez-faire*
('atomism'). In the case of welfare this means a position akin to the
'institutional' pattern. It is primarily the two extremes, the middle class
and the communist societies that move towards the middle ground. In
the former, *laissez-faire* and market-based distribution is gradually
superseded by a measure of state responsibility and provision for basic
needs while in the latter, total state control over resources and their
distribution gives way to a more pluralistic arrangement.

What are the grounds for believing that a 'mixed' system fits the conditions of advanced industrialism best? The answer, in a nutshell, is that on the one hand, the 'complexity of the fully developed industrial society requires, in the name of efficiency and initiative, a degree of decentralisation of control', while at the same time it also requires 'a large measure of central control by the state'.[9] It is as 'utopian' to expect that a mature industrial society can survive the stresses and strains generated by *laissez-faire* as it is to expect that under communism the state will 'wither away'. Given the scale, complexity and interdependence between groups and institutions characteristic of industrial society, the state becomes and must remain the key regulatory agency. The integration of society around the dominant values must remain a prime function of the state. The social services perform an important part of this function. But the productive enterprise, the firm, also has 'a dominant position under pluralistic industrialism'. Indeed Kerr asserts that the 'responsibility for guaranteeing the minimum welfare and security of industrial man rests in large measure upon his managers and his government'.[10] Irrespective of the political system of industrial society, then, both the state and the enterprise will play a prominent part in meeting basic needs. We have seen already why the state emerges as a key institution as far as welfare is concerned. But what of the enterprise? Its importance derives chiefly from the centrality of work – of the production of goods and services – in industrial society. It is the enterprise that organises production. On it devolves the task of bringing men and material together, of motivating men, of maintaining a reasonably committed and efficient labour force. Furthermore, in conditions of advanced industrialisation, the scale of operation of the enterprise is large and tends to grow bigger. Because of its size, scale of operation and investment and the like, the enterprise possesses the necessary resources as well as the motivation for developing schemes of welfare. Welfare structures of an earlier age – friendly societies, co-operatives, charities, trade union benefits – can hardly match the capacity of either the state or the enterprise to mobilise resources and to underwrite expensive schemes of welfare. There are, however, other reasons why the enterprise becomes more 'welfare-conscious'. Compared to the early phases of industrialisation, labour becomes a far scarcer and more important productive resource. The development and maintenance of an efficient work force thus becomes a key imperative. These then are some of the

For love segmented into next divisions. Over-simplifies the [illegible] model [illegible] to enable this division

38   *Approaches to Welfare*

main reasons why the enterprise emerges as a leading partner of the state in the 'business' of welfare. Generalising for the capitalist countries as a whole, we might say that in the course of transition from early to advanced industrialisation, the welfare system changes from a predominantly 'residual' to an 'institutional' type.

In communist countries too the movement is towards the middle ground but from an opposite direction. Communists begin with a strong commitment to state collectivism and egalitarianism. But as advanced stages of industrial development are reached it becomes clear that total state control and bureaucratic management are not very helpful in running a mass consumption economy efficiently. Indeed, a measure of decentralisation of production as well as consumption becomes highly desirable. Advanced communist countries are therefore likely to relax state collectivism somewhat and permit some development of market and other forms of social provision, especially enterprise welfare. In short a measure of pluralism is likely to develop within the broad framework of a state controlled system of distribution and welfare.[11]

To sum up: the theory tries to explain the differing social policies in the early stages of industrialisation primarily in terms of the nature of dominant elites or social classes and their ideologies. In more advanced stages of industrialisation, however, it believes that the functional necessities of industrialism are such as to impose similar policies on all societies. The result is not that industrial societies become alike but that differences narrow appreciably. Ideology does not end but there is a withering away of extremist ideologies and institutions – a mellowing which pushes towards the centre. In other words, as far as social policy is concerned, *laissez-faire* and total state collectivism tend to be replaced by a form of 'institutional' pattern.

What is 'centre' = mixed? Is this really a compromise?

Technological Determinism: An Assessment   *No way.*

How adequate is convergence theory in explaining the relationship between society and social policy? Let us begin by looking at some of its advantages over citizenship theory. We have noted already that its scope is wider. Its interpretation of welfare is not restricted to a particular country or even to Western societies. Nor is it concerned with statutory welfare alone. Thus the theory takes note of occupational or enterprise-based welfare as an important element in modern social

Still no details of egs. of this sort of welfare ~~expendite~~ expenditu

policy and seeks to explain this in terms of the logic of advanced industrialism. But its main superiority over citizenship theory lies in its social structural character. It explains the differences in social policy in industrial societies, albeit for the initial stages alone, in terms of dominant social groups and their ideologies. More generally, it tries to explain developments in policy in relation to some of the basic features of industrial society, e.g. the scale and complexity of social organisation, the centrality of the goals of economic and industrial development, geographical and occupational mobility and its consequences for the family and community. In the social structural character of its explanation it represents a major advance over citizenship theory. Its notion of 'stages' in the development of industrial society is also useful in suggesting the relevance of particular social priorities, resources and organisations (e.g. friendly societies) at a particular level of economic development. Undoubtedly the periodisation of social development presents many problems, but at least potentially it seems a fruitful way of exploring the relation between social structure and social policy in industrialised societies.

There is, none the less, a great deal in the theory that is open to criticism. Perhaps the first point to be made is its deterministic mode of analysis. Indeed, the idea of inevitability underlying the theory is bound to repel those who see social policy largely in terms of values and choices. For, the claim that everything is already decided in advance by the nature of modern technology and economy denies the very possibility of a 'policy' about anything, social or otherwise, since policy presupposes the act of deliberation and choice. To be fair, however, the problem of determinism is not peculiar to convergence theory. There are deeply deterministic elements in Marxist analysis too. Indeed sociological explanations generally imply a degree of 'constraint' – a determinate relationship between variables (for example between social class and educational achievement). Clearly, no one can deny the element of constraint in social life. Decision-making and choice is never completely 'free'. The relation between man and society is one of relative freedom, of relative constraint, and it is wrong to pose the problem as one of either total determinism or totally free choice. Rather it is necessary to look at the constraints present in any given situation in terms of major pressures and influences which limit choice. The understanding of a determinate relationship must therefore leave open the possibility of influencing and changing the rela-

Over-antonomizes the perspectives
I doesn't say who we are but this about. Where all the ofp.

Why?

tionship (e.g. weakening the association between class and education through policies of positive discrimination). Earlier we criticised social administration (see p. 14) for ignoring the relevance of structural factors – the dominant values and institutions of capitalism, for example – for the exercise of choice in social policy. In the case of convergence theory the opposite stricture would apply. It leans too far in the direction of determinism, ignoring alternatives and the element of choice in social life.

However, even if we reject determinism it is still necessary to examine the nature of the constraining influences suggested by the theory. Put simply, the question is how useful and valid is the stress on technology and economy? As neither social administration nor citizenship, the two perspectives examined earlier, gives much importance to the influence of technology on social policy, the stress on this factor is welcome. What is objectionable however is that in the name of technological imperatives, the theory virtually denies the influence of all other factors. Although at least one major version of the theory of industrialism (the one we have examined) fully recognises the influence of culture, ideology, elites and the like in the making of social policy, this is held to be true of the initial stages of industrialisation only. Later the functional necessities are supposed to take over and dominate the scene increasingly. Clearly, this assertion is unwarranted, for neither reasoning nor evidence lends it much support. There are no good grounds to suppose that advanced industrial society spells the end of ideology – that culture, political beliefs, class interests, historical continuities and the like cease to influence social structure.[12] Nor does evidence bear out the thesis of increasing similarity of social policy to any great extent. Looking at the patterns of welfare in advanced industrial countries what we find is a measure of both similarity and difference and little evidence of the latter disappearing.[13] True, a 'weak' thesis of convergence can be sustained; thus in all Western industrial countries the state has assumed greater responsibility for meeting needs and occupational welfare has also become more prominent. But this still leaves scope for a great deal of diversity in welfare patterns, for example in respect of the mix between these two types of provision. And the mix matters, unless we consider these provisions as functional equivalents (which clearly they are not).[14] Indeed differences which may seem minor in the context of a very general and formal theory such as convergence may be of considerable importance from the viewpoint of welfare. The fact that the state has assumed basic responsibility for education in all industrial societies does not mean that the scope of state activity in education, the nature of educational organisation and provision (selective or otherwise, or the availability of student grants, for example) and the like have become or are becoming identical. In the context of welfare, these are not details that can be ignored as irrelevant. Thus Titmuss's study of blood transfusion services in industrialised countries[15] shows important variations (and little sign of convergence) despite the fact that in virtually all the industrial countries he examined, with the exception of the United States, the state has assumed basic responsibility for medical care. In other words, the level of generality – the focus on the broad structural pattern – at which theories such as convergence are pitched tends to be high. This limits their relevance to a humanistic study of welfare.

If we reject technological and economic determinism in an extreme form then we are left with a theory which stresses the influence of industrial technology and economy, as one among other factors, in the shaping of social policy. In this form the theory is far more acceptable. Even so it must be emphasised that technology does not determine social action directly. Its influence is indirect; it is mediated through political and ideological structures. Thus, serious accidents at work may be the result of industrial technology. But this in itself does not make industrial injury a social problem requiring government intervention. A social problem implies an 'objective' condition (accidents due to the use of industrial machinery) plus evaluation. Technological and economic factors often explain the former but never the latter. And here we come to a major criticism of the explanation of social policy development offered by this theory. By connecting the social structure with industrialism in a general functionalist manner it fails to account for the human and social processes involved in change and development. The social groups and classes involved in the process of defining and articulating a problem, the underlying values and ideologies, the nature of conflicts and compromises, the vested interests that have to be overcome in the course of the development of social policy are all left out of the explanation. What must be recognised, however, is that these are largely sins of omission; they do not necessarily invalidate the theory. Rather they draw attention to its limitations. As Goldthorpe has stressed, a highly generalised explanation of development of this kind needs to be supplemented with more detailed, action-centred accounts.[16] Finally we may note that in so far as the theory lacks a group-action perspective and plays down the role of ideologies and beliefs as well as of conflict, it shares a common approach to social change with the citizenship school. As regards implications for policy, however, it differs a good deal from the latter. Unlike citizenship theory it has no basic concept concerned with the development of social policy. Since policy is seen as an adjunct to industrial development virtually everything that happens appears as necessary and inevitable; the theory offers no guide to action, except perhaps in its endorsement of the institutional pattern of welfare as the most 'appropriate' for advanced industrial society. In sum, the reservations and qualifications outlined above weaken the theory a good deal. None the less the relation between industrialisation, society and welfare suggested by the theory can be seen as a useful model – an abstraction against which to study the actual processes of development.

Chapter 4

The Functionalist View

Students of social policy may be inclined to see the functionalist view of welfare as identical with the perspective outlined in the previous chapter. But there is more to functionalism than the idea that institutions develop out of necessity. Its basic propositions therefore merit close attention. The principal tenets of a school of thought are not easy to specify, but two basic features seem common to a wide variety of 'functionalisms'. First, the conception of society as a system – a set of inter-related patterns which constitute the 'parts' of an integrated 'whole' (society is seen as analogous to an organism). Secondly, the analysis of these patterns – social institutions – in terms of their 'function', i.e. the contribution they make towards the efficient working of the 'whole'. Given this basic approach, much of functionalist analysis concerns itself with, for example, specifying the functions that must be performed if a society is to survive, studying the functional division of labour among the institutions of society, and examining the inter-relationship between various institutional patterns from the viewpoint of 'good fit' or harmony.

The Nature of Welfare and Its Development

(a) Classical functionalists The use of the part-whole analogy and of
the notion of function in the analysis of society – an approach
variously known as 'organicism', 'holism' or in modern terminology
'systems analysis' – is as old as social thought itself. Elements of functionalist thinking are to be found in many social theorists of the for-
mative period of sociological thought, for example Montesquieu,
Comte, Spencer, Durkheim and Pareto. However, if Spencer with his
organicism and evolutionary view of social development stands closest
to functionalism, the founders of modern functionalism have been influenced far more by Durkheim.[1]

What, if anything, have Spencer and Durkheim to say about social
welfare institutions? Understandably enough, their theoretical writing
is not directly concerned with the analysis of welfare.[2] Spencer, it is
true, wrote extensively on questions of social policy but chiefly as a
polemicist. A bitter opponent of state intervention, he was mainly concerned with defending a *laissez-faire* social policy. But his polemics
were largely the value judgements of a Non-conformist radical. In any
case, the connection between his sociological theory and value
judgements is, at best, slight.[3] The arguments adduced by Spencer
against state intervention, especially in connection with social welfare,
do not now seem novel although they are not without contemporary
relevance.[4] In any case they have little to do with the sociological
analysis, the understanding, of welfare. In his obsession with up-
holding the virtues of *laissez-faire*, Spencer's politics and ethics got
the better of his social analysis. He did little to explain the nature of
social welfare institutions in past and present societies. Yet as we shall
see from Durkheim's approach to the question, and even more from
that of contemporary functionalist theory, such an explanation is implicit in Spencer's organicist view of society.

Unlike Spencer, Durkheim was not opposed to state intervention in
principle. In any case if as a social philosopher he had reservations
about the increasing scope of state activity, as a social scientist he
could not ignore it as a fact. He recognised that the growing volume of
state activity in the regulation of social and economic life was in ac-
cord with the (functionalist) view of social development to which both
he and Spencer subscribed. The increasing scale and complexity of the
modern social structure requires a correspondingly large amount of

co-ordination and regulation. And this, notes Durkheim, tends to devolve upon the central organ of society – the state. As we reach the 'higher' type of society, writes Durkheim, 'A multitude of functions which were diffuse become concentrated. The care of educating the young, of protecting public health, of presiding over the ways of administering public aid, of administering the means of transport and communication, little by little move over into the sphere of the central organ.'[5] Durkheim takes Spencer to task for regarding big government as an aberration, as a pathological phenomenon resulting from the 'concourse of accidental circumstances'. For Durkheim the increasing 'dimensions of the governmental organ' was a perfectly normal, evolutionary development.[6]

Durkheim rejects Spencer's utilitarian and contractual view of the foundations of the social order in 'industrial' society. While agreeing with Spencer that in modern society social harmony comes essentially from the division of labour, that is from specialisation and interdependence, Durkheim rejects the notion that the free play of individual interests is a sufficient basis of social solidarity. For even a complex society, with a highly developed division of labour, is not merely 'a jumble of juxtaposed atoms, between which it can establish only external, transient contacts'.[7] Rather, what is involved is reciprocity and mutuality, 'a complex of obligations' from which we cannot free ourselves. And in modern society, observes Durkheim, it is increasingly the state which is entrusted with 'the duty of reminding us of the sentiment of common solidarity'.[8] In so far as all societies, including the modern ones, are also moral communities, they are not without collective sentiments and the bond of solidarity. Hence altruism, writes Durkheim, 'is not destined to become, as Spencer desires, a sort of agreeable ornament to social life, but it will forever be its fundamental basis. How can we ever really dispense with it? . . . Wherever there are societies, there is altruism, because there is solidarity.'[9]

However, what exercised Durkheim most was the tendency towards 'anomie' in modern society – the absence of a moral force sufficiently strong and authoritative to restrain and stabilise the individual and through him the social order. He did not believe that the modern state – too big and remote an institution and more a servant than a master of the people – could provide it.[10] Unlike Spencer, Durkheim believed in social regulation, in constraining the individual in the interests of his own and the common good. He recognised that modern societies could not achieve solidarity without attending to the problem of social justice. But his main concern was with restraining men's desires and needs rather than with their fulfilment. Not poverty but dissatisfaction with poverty – the absence of contentment with one's lot – was for Durkheim the major problem of the day.[11] Durkheim's attitude to the state is not easy to summarise. But if as a social scientist he accepted growing state action – the position of the state as a repository of the community's values and obligations – as a social philosopher he was not enamoured of increasing reliance on the state. For a moral force, effective in regulating individual desires and actions, Durkheim looked towards occupational and professional guilds. At least some of the welfare functions were to be discharged by these organisations, working in conjunction with the state.[12]

From the viewpoint of the sociological analysis of welfare, Durkheim's value judgements concerning social organisation and his prescriptions relevant to welfare are less important than his general theoretical orientation. His stress on the collectivity (as opposed to Spencer's individualism), his appreciation of the expanding scope of state activity in sociological terms, his emphasis on solidarity as a prerequisite of all societal communities brings him close to suggesting the links between welfare and a functionalist view of society. But Durkheim stops short of spelling out these connections and, as with Spencer, his theoretical standpoint becomes more directly relevant to the analysis of welfare in the form of modern functionalism. It is to this that we must now turn.

(b) Modern Functionalists For the basic ideas of modern sociological functionalism we draw chiefly on the works of three contemporary theorists – Parsons, Merton and Smelser. Parsons and Merton are leading exponents of functionalism while Smelser, a collaborator of Parsons, has written on themes relevant to social welfare.[13] However, it must be made clear at the outset that none of these sociologists are *directly* concerned with the analysis of social welfare albeit both Parsons and Smelser have paid some attention to the subject. What follows, therefore, is more in the nature of an interpretation based on functionalist theory rather than an examination of what these sociologists have actually said about social welfare.

(i) *Welfare as Integration: Functional Prerequisites*

Parsons has suggested that the survival of a society (or any social system) may be thought of as being conditional upon four functional requirements being met successfully: adaptation, goal attainment, integration and pattern-maintenance. The first refers, broadly, to economic tasks; the second to political ones; the third is concerned with maintaining harmony and solidarity; and the fourth with the continuation of basic value patterns. For Parsons these four are the basic functional elements (sub-systems) of a society.[14] A particular social organisation (a school, a church, a hospital, for example) or a social institution (education or religion) may be concerned primarily with one of these tasks but most institutions are involved in all four. The institution of welfare, according to the functionalists, primarily belongs to the third, the integrative sub-system. Integration – the process which makes a social system more cohesive, the relation between the component parts more harmonious – may be of two kinds: system integration and social integration.[15] The former refers to the integration of institutions, the latter to that of social groups. Although the distinction is largely analytic, integration in one sense does not necessarily imply integration in the other. Let us look at an example of system integration. If, say, the economy needs a well-educated labour force but the educational system is so organised that a great deal of educational talent is wasted then, clearly, these two parts of society – the economic and the educational – are not in harmony. They are malintegrated. A change in educational (or economic) values and organisation is necessary to correct the imbalance. Much of the public provision of education in Britain and associated reforms can be seen as attempts to correct imbalances of this nature, that is, to achieve system integration. Social integration, on the other hand, involves the reduction of conflict between social groups – workers and management, Catholics and Protestants, etc. It is concerned with enhancing morale, commitment and loyalty towards a collectivity on the part of its members. Put simply, system integration is concerned with the 'instrumental' aspects of a collectivity, i.e. with efficiency; social integration with its 'expressive' aspects, i.e. with morale and cohesiveness.

But why should integration be a general necessity, a function that is essential for the survival (or effectiveness) of all communities and therefore cannot easily be ignored? The answer, implicit in the functionalist argument, is two-fold: first, it is obvious that in order to survive as a going concern, a collectivity – be it nation-state, firm, trade union or club – must try to keep the levels of disequilibrium and conflict between its component 'parts' (whether thought of as institutions or as groups and individuals) as low as possible. In the interests of effective functioning of the system, dissension and disharmony must be kept in check. Hence, 'social control' or the need to maintain order forms a part of social integration. The social control aspect of integration is concerned less with creating a sense of community or enhancing solidarity and more with ensuring that the established patterns or arrangements are not disrupted and that social peace is maintained. Thus functionalist theory suggests that maintaining order is a *leitmotif* of a good deal of 'welfare' activity. In sum, then, the integrative institutions are important partly because they contribute towards efficiency, stability and order.

Second, any society or other collectivity which has the character of a community – that is its members share and wish to share a sense of belonging – must have some sentiments of solidarity. This means that institutions and practices which express altruism – a concern for members of the community – tend to be a normal feature of societies. In this sense social welfare institutions are both a cause as well as a consequence of community. For if the act of recognising and meeting individual needs enhances solidarity, such an act implies solidarity – the sense of being part of a community. This communal character of welfare is evident in its underlying principle, namely that individuals have a claim on the community's resources not because they have 'earned' it ('desert') but because solidarity enjoins that their wants be recognised and met ('need'). Here the model of social relation is the same as that found in family and kinship institutions, i.e. based on affective ties and values.

(ii) *The Development of Welfare*

What is the relation between social structure and welfare? How is change in one related to change in the other? For functionalists the key concept in the analysis of social development is 'structural differentiation'. Briefly, it is the notion that development consists in the movement of societies from a simple (undifferentiated) to a complex (highly differentiated) type of social structure. The four functional tasks (mentioned above), however, are essentially the same for all human societies and do not change. What changes primarily is the structure – the nature of institutional arrangements through which the different functions are performed. The structure becomes more specialised: in the course of social development, a multi-functional institutional structure splits up into several structures each with a more specialised function.[17] This differentiation of structures results in various imbalances and malintegration, a condition which requires new forms of integration. Paradoxically, this in turn produces more specialised structures. As Smelser puts it, 'Development proceeds as a contrapuntal interplay between differentiation (which is divisive of established society) and integration (which unites differentiated structures on a new basis).'[18] Take, for example, the change from domestic or household industry to factory production. The separation of production from kinship structure, according to Smelser,

> immediately creates integrative problems. How is information concerning employment opportunities to be conveyed to work people? How are the interests of families to be integrated with the interests of firms? How are families to be protected from market fluctuations? Whereas such integrative exigencies were faced by kinsmen, neighbours, and local largesse in pre-modern settings, development gives birth to dozens of institutions and organizations geared to these new integrative problems – labour recruitment agencies and exchanges, labour unions, government regulation of labour allocation, welfare and relief arrangements, co-operation societies, and savings institutions.[19]

This is fairly typical of how functionalists see the process of differentiation. But it may be useful to take a brief look at the functionalist view of social development, from primitive through to industrial societies, in relation to welfare.

In primitive (tribal) societies there are no specialised patterns, no formal organisations concerned with meeting needs. Needs are met, to a greater or lesser extent, through the kinship and community structure. For example, rules of reciprocity among kinsmen ensure a rough and ready equality of distribution – resources are shared more or less equitably among members of a clan or a village so that basic needs are met.[20] In short, kinship is the basic institution concerned with welfare (as well as with many other functions) in primitive societies.

With social and economic advancement specialised structures – political, religious, military, economic, welfare – develop for handling the vastly enlarged scope of the four basic functions. Thus in complex pre-industrial societies, the family and kin group remains an important structure of support for the individual. In addition, however, we find charitable organisations, various formal and informal relief arrangements made by local communities (village, parish) as well as occupational communities (craft and merchant guilds, for example) ministering to the welfare of the needy. But, above all, religious organisations play a major part in the provision of welfare at this stage of social development, for in these societies it is precisely religion – both as a set of beliefs and as an organisation – that symbolises and upholds the idea of community. Unlike in primitive societies, religion is no longer fused with the kinship structure, and the sense of community – both in respect of identity and sentiments – revolves round religious beliefs, symbols and practices. Caring for the poor, the sick and the needy; exhorting the fortunate to give alms, to remember their duty towards their less fortunate brethren; organising help and in general keeping alive the sense of community; these are integrative functions *par excellence* which devolve upon the religious organisations in agrarian society.[21] Indeed, religious organisations have traditionally (and successfully) combined the twin functions of social integration – instilling and enhancing the sense of community and solidarity among believers (irrespective of rank) – and the maintenance of social control – reconciling individuals to existing values and institutions so that social peace is not disturbed. Compared to primitive societies, then, the structures concerned with meeting needs become rather more formal and specialised in advanced pre-industrial societies, and religion tends to be the key social organisation concerned with welfare.

With further socio-economic advance, leading to the industrial society, institutional specialisation develops further. Societal scale and complexity increases. So does mobility – both geographical and occupational. The extended family and the local community weaken as collectivities. Religious organisations weaken in their hold over society (secularisation) and hence in their capacity to act as integrative institutions. More specialised structures arise to cope with the growing volume of welfare functions. Organised and specialised charities of various kinds proliferate. So do voluntary associations – friendly societies and the like. Moreover, two new patterns of welfare develop in industrial society, namely the social services and benefits provided by the enterprise, with the former tending to be the principal institution concerned with meeting needs. Although the techniques and many of the needs met through these arrangements are novel and related to industrialism, taken in a generic sense the institutions of welfare perform a broadly integrative function, essentially not dissimilar to that in less developed societies. This completes our outline of the functionalist view of welfare and its development. How valid and useful a perspective is it?

The Functionalist View: An Assessment

(a) The Concept of Welfare In functionalism we have a theory purporting to be universal in scope. Unlike the perspectives outlined earlier, functionalism is not concerned with a particular country or type of society but with society in general. Its conception of welfare reflects this universality, and in our view it is in this that the great merit of the functionalist concept lies. By relating welfare to an element of social life (integration and community) that is universal, it offers a view of welfare that is social in a fundamental sense. In place of various *ad hoc* approaches – for example, equating welfare with the social services or with citizenship – it restores welfare to its legitimate place as a part of every society, a social element as universal as education or religion. The functionalist notion of welfare is not confined to the societal or nation-state level. Society is only the highest form of collectivity. In a complex society many other social collectivities exist, e.g. business firms, armed forces, ethnic and occupational communities. To a varying degree, and in some form or another, patterns of welfare can be seen as a feature of any collectivity with a communal character. This generalised notion of welfare can thus encompass social services, enterprise welfare, charitable and voluntary as well as mutual aid of various kinds. However, this very generality of the concept – centred around the notion of integration – lays it open to the charge of vagueness. Indeed, in functionalist literature the notion of integration has been used very loosely and there are few social institutions that do not take on an integrative character. To be fair,

however, it must be said that broad generalisations of this kind, in this case involving the society-welfare relationship, cannot be precise in their empirical reference. Even Titmuss, hardly given to obscurantist thinking, finds it difficult to generalise in precise terms about the subject matter of social administration. 'Its primary areas of unifying interest', writes Titmuss, 'are centred in those social institutions that foster integration and discourage alienation.' [22] This definition focuses on social integration but the idea of welfare as system integration is by no means absent from Titmuss's writings. Indeed the distinction between these two major objectives (and consequences) of social policy is itself an enormously useful contribution to come out of functional analysis, although its analytic potential is yet to be exploited. Moreover, by linking the notion of 'community' or 'solidarity' (the one presupposes the other) with welfare, the analysis draws attention to both an important source of 'altruistic' action as well as to one of its main consequences. Finally, let us note that the ideas of community, integration and the structural specialisation of societies enable the theory to explain the role of religion in welfare in a way that none of the perspectives outlined earlier can.

All the same this notion of welfare remains one-sided. Based on a unitary view of society (looking at society as a whole), it overlooks the fact that social policies have functions (consequences) not only for society or for the system as a whole but also for the 'parts', i.e. for different groups and institutions that go to make up society. What may be good and integrative for society as a whole may have quite disintegrative consequences for the parts or at least for some of them. Thus Young and Willmott's classic study of kinship in Bethnal Green showed that one consequence of local authority housing policy was to disrupt the extended family and kin network. [23] What was an integrative measure from the society's viewpoint (helping less well-off families with housing) was disruptive from the view point of extended kin and community relations. Merton, a leading functionalist, has introduced the idea of 'dysfunction' to take such distinctions into account. [24] In short, Merton recognises that the consequences of a social pattern need not be entirely 'positive' or beneficial for the system: there may also be 'negative' consequences or dysfunctions. Items may be functional for some groups, institutions or value systems and dysfunctional for others. [25] However, once the unitary view of society is abandoned, the concept of 'function' becomes almost redundant. Instead we have to think in terms of the 'consequences' of social measures for specific groups and institutions as well as from the viewpoint of a particular kind of society or social system.

But to do this is to recognise that human societies (or other collectivities) are characterised by unity as well as diversity, consensus as well as conflict. From here it is only a short step to admitting that coercion often plays an important part in maintaining cohesion. But this viewpoint cannot easily be accommodated within the functionalist view of society, based on the analogy of an organic or a mechanical system. This analogy is limiting in two ways. First, it does not allow conflict and coercion to be thought of as an essential part of social organisation. The result is a consensus view of society. Second, it prevents functionalists from recognising the fact that unlike organic or mechanical systems, societies are made and maintained by individuals (actors) who have values, interests, purpose and the like and that these must be brought into the analysis.

A second problem arising out of the functionalist approach is that the idea of function or consequence makes no distinction between the intentions of actors and the actual results of social action. Yet the distinction is important. Again, Merton has come to the rescue by drawing a distinction between manifest and latent function or intended and unintended consequences of social action.[26] To make this distinction, however, is to recognise that social institutions, e.g. the social services, have multiple consequences. And this weakens further the case for defining social policy in terms of the function of integration alone. However that may be, the distinction between intended and unintended consequences is of the utmost importance in social analysis, for it draws attention to connections between social phenomena which may not be obvious but whose effects may yet be far-reaching. Weber's study of the consequences of calvinistic beliefs for the development of capitalism is of course a classic example.[27] An example less dramatic but more relevant to welfare has been mentioned already, namely the unintended consequences of housing policy for kinship networks. In reality a neat separation between 'intended' and 'unintended' consequences cannot always be made. None the less the principle behind the distinction remains valid.

The study of the consequences of social policy is central to social administration. And sociologically-orientated scholars, e.g. Titmuss, have never tired of drawing attention to the unintended or unrecognised consequences of social policy.[28] However, in the interventionist framework of social administration, attention is naturally focused on the intended consequences – on assessing whether the aims of social policy have been realised. Moreover, social administration's central concern – the welfare of the individual – as well as its multi-disciplinary approach limits its scope for exploring the wider ramifications of social policy. Perhaps the 'sociology of welfare' is a more suitable context for such explorations.

Another problem of functional analysis is concerned with the question of variations in welfare patterns. We have seen earlier that functionalist theory suggests a correspondence between institutions of welfare and levels of social development. Thus kinship is concerned with welfare in primitive societies, religion in advanced pre-industrial societies, and the state in industrial societies. The problem, however, arises with explaining differences in welfare among societies at the same level of development. In industrial societies generally, the state tends to play a prominent part in welfare. None the less important differences do exist in this respect among industrial countries, for example between the United States and the U.S.S.R. How can the theory account for such differences? Merton's answer to this problem is the notion of 'functional alternatives',[29] whereby the same functions can be performed by a range of institutions (though this range is not unlimited); hence the variation. But this weakens the functionalist equation of a particular level of social development with the predominance of a particular institution – for example that of state welfare in industrial society. In any case, the concept of functional alternatives cannot 'explain' differences in social policy, for what needs explanation is not so much the fact of variation itself as the nature – the substance – of these variations. But here functionalism reaches the limit of its explanatory potential. It cannot explain why one pattern exists rather than another for the simple reason that without a perspective which can take account of the major social groups and their inter-relation in terms of the conflict of interests, values and beliefs, these differences cannot be explained. In any case, the very notion of functional alternatives seems of doubtful validity, for it implies that differences between structures of welfare do not matter as the latter are merely different ways of doing the same thing. From this viewpoint, the Victorian Poor Law and modern social services would not seem very different: both were concerned with integration, social control and so on. At any rate functionalism does not seem to have a concept which can distinguish between these two types of social policy adequately.

Perhaps the weakness of the idea of functional alternatives can be better illustrated with reference to statutory and enterprise welfare – two contemporary forms of social provision that may seem equivalent. Let us look at some of the obvious differences between the two. The enterprise is a part of the market structure; its social benefits, like other rewards, tend to reflect the occupational hierarchy. The social services on the other hand, are based on some notion of equity between citizens. Again, the benefits provided vary from one enterprise to another because of differences in policy, resources, etc. Social services, by contrast, provide uniform benefits. In one case we have differentiation and in the other standardisation. In fact these two types of welfare differ in other, significant, ways (see chapter 6). Moreover the wider, unintended consequences of each are also likely to be different. Thus we can only treat these structures as equivalent if we focus on some very generalised similarity of function – meeting needs, for example – and ignore significant differences.

This is not to suggest, however, that the notion of functional alternatives should be discarded. It is a useful concept in so far as it draws attention to a broad functional similarity between social patterns which may otherwise seem disparate. This stress on function rather than structural setting is of considerable value in social analysis.[30] In support of this we could perhaps cite Titmuss's pathbreaking analysis which showed basic functional similarity between three disparate structures, namely the social services, fiscal benefits and enterprise welfare.[31] It is important to bear in mind, however, that functional similarity should be understood as similarity from a particular viewpoint only. In other respects the structures may differ quite significantly. It is when this distinction is glossed over, as in functional analysis generally, that the notion of functional alternatives can be seriously misleading.

(b) The Development of Welfare: Structural Differentiation The limitations of the functionalist approach are nowhere more evident than in its explanation of the development of welfare, for its master concept of change, namely structural differentiation, does not so much explain, as describe the process of development from the viewpoint of increasing specialisation of structures (and functions). Leaving the

question of explanation aside for the moment, how valid is this description? Undoubtedly, increasing specialisation – of roles, organisations and patterns – is a feature of social development generally and welfare is no exception. Thus if we look at the development of the social services in Britain from the nineteenth century to the present day we can see a gradual specialisation of services, organisations and workers. The Poor Law service with its mixed general workhouse and the general relieving officer has given way to a variety of services as well as to specialised organisations – children's homes, general hospitals, hospitals for the mentally subnormal, old people's homes, etc. – and specialist social workers – children's officers, mental health officers, psychiatric social workers and others. However, increased specialisation is neither inevitable nor desirable. Indeed there is a subsidiary trend of development concerned with reversing the process of specialisation. Thus the move towards a generic training course and a common professional identity of social work is an attempt to do away with forms of specialisation whose rationale is little more than historical accident. It is true that functionalists see the process of differentiation as causing 'strains', 'imbalances', etc. so that it is followed by forms of integration.[32] No doubt, some of the developments aimed at countering the effects of excessive specialisation can be seen in these terms. More importantly, however, to see the development of welfare merely as a multiplication of roles and organisations is to miss out an important, indeed a vital, part of the story. Thus the move from the Poor Law to the modern social services has entailed changes of other kinds, notably in the substance of social policy. In short, social policy development, as indeed other forms of development, is not only about increasing specialisation but also about changes in values and beliefs, in income, status and power of various social groups and in the life-chances of individuals. Unfortunately the functionalist cannot catch any of this rich substance of social change in his theoretical net of structural differentiation.

What is more, in seeing change simply as adaptation – some form of reflex action on the part of the social organism – functionalism fails to offer a meaningful account of the mechanism, of the human processes, involved in the differentiation of structures and their subsequent reintegration. Typical of the idea of an automatic response is the statement that 'development *gives birth to* [my italics] dozens of

institutions and organisations geared to ... integrative problems'.[33]
How these organisations are 'born', what 'labour pains' they undergo,
what social groups, values and conflicts are involved in the process
forms no part of functionalist explanation. In short, functionalism can
neither explain the differences in welfare provisions among societies at
a similar level of development (as we have seen above), nor has it the
resources for explaining the process of development in any meaningful
sense. (The stumbling block, once again, is the organic analogy (or
what amounts to the same thing, the consensus view of society) and its
corollary, the virtual absence of a group or action perspective. This is
where, as we shall see later, the Marxist approach, extended to include
not only the major social classes and their conflict but social groups
more generally, can form a powerful complement to the functionalist
view of the specialisation of welfare functions. Thus the Poor Law reform of 1834, a landmark in the development of social policy in early
industrial Britain, can hardly be explained in functionalist terms.
True, the administrative aspects of these reforms – the enlargement of
the local unit of administration, central supervision and control, appointment of full-time officials and the like – do fit the functionalist
scheme of development quite well.[34] But as regards the substance of
the change, the Poor Law policy itself, functionalism can say little.
Marxian class analysis, on the other hand, would have little to say
about the 'modernisation' of the Poor Law structure but a great deal
about the substance of these reforms. What is missing in the functionalist concept of welfare is the class dimension, the link with
stratification – with inequality, domination and social control understood from a social class standpoint. This is a dimension that
Marxism provides. Without it we can hardly claim to have
'understood' the nature and development of welfare, for example the
English Poor Laws or Bismarck's social legislation. The history of
social welfare cannot be seen merely as a story of increasing institutional complexity and specialisation of tasks, of increasing interdependence. It is also a story of social inequality and potential or actual
conflict around it. If welfare has to do with community and cohesion
it has also to do with class interests, inequality and conflict. Indeed,
even structural differentiation and integration involves vested interests
and is far from a smooth process. However, even if these substantive differences (and changes) in welfare patterns are recognised
and their significance appreciated, there still remains the problem of

explanation. And this can hardly be attempted without reference to actors (at least collective ones, i.e. groups), their beliefs and values, interests and the like which remains a major lacuna in the functionalist approach.

(c) Implications for policy The link between theoretical standpoints and their practical implications is rarely self-evident or unambiguous. Thus both Durkheim and Spencer take a broadly organicist view of society. But whereas Spencer invokes the idea of social evolution to support a *laissez-faire* policy, Durkheim finds the growing structural complexity of society an ample justification for state intervention. However, despite the difficulty of establishing a correspondence between theory and policy an attempt must be made to single out what seem to be the most obvious implications.

First, Merton's strictures about dysfunction notwithstanding, functional analysis tends to see social institutions primarily in terms of their 'positive' contribution. The tendency is to see every existing institution or pattern as in some sense beneficial for the society 'as a whole'. This results in a sort of justification of, or at least an uncritical attitude towards, the *status quo*. The prime example of this is the notorious functionalist attempt to explain inequality in terms of its positive functions for society, namely to provide necessary incentives (material and social) for work and achievement.[35] In this analysis, the dysfunctions of inequality were conveniently forgotten. Secondly, with a consensus view of society functionalism can scarcely avoid identifying, however unintentionally, with the ruling powers. Thus seemingly neutral concepts like 'integration' and 'social control' serve to conceal the question of power, of class relations and inequality involved in different forms of social policy. Thirdly, modern functionalism perhaps epitomises the scientism and the so-called 'value-free' approach characteristic of the social sciences. The result is that its major concepts do not help in the critical evaluation of social institutions. And this limits the uses of functionalism from the standpoint of the evaluation and formulation of social policy.

There is a good deal in the functionalist approach that lends itself to a critique of *laissez-faire* and to support for a collectivist social policy, but this potential has rarely been explored. This may be, in part, due to sociologists' lack of concern with questions of policy. Let us look at two examples. First, Durkheim's concept of anomie. Durkheim was much concerned with the tendency towards anomie, i.e. the absence of sufficient social and moral regulation (and hence of stability) in modern society. In particular, he singled out economic *laissez-faire* as a prime example of this anomie.[36] Durkheim's focus is more often on the anomic individual (in need of restraint), but his concern with the social conditions which produce anomie cannot be questioned. Although he looked to occupational associations or guilds rather than to the state for a solution of this problem, it should be remembered that in Durkheim's scheme of things the state and the occupational corporations were to work together in creating a more stable and harmonious society. At any rate, as Horton has pointed out, Durkheim's concept of anomie contains a powerful critique (at least implicitly, though at times it is quite explicit) of the economic and social aspects of *laissez-faire* capitalism.[37] But modern functionalists have failed to develop this side of anomie. On the whole they have not taken sufficient notice of the fact that in many ways the welfare state has mitigated the economically generated anomie in modern capitalist society or at least has the potential to do so.[38] It does this in at least two ways: first, by regulating and stabilising economic life; and second, by attending to the problem of social justice – one of the key elements in maintaining cohesion and stability in modern society.

The second example is concerned with the importance accorded by functionalists to the family and to its role in the process of socialisation.[39] This emphasis on the family (especially on the nuclear family as the form of family which 'fits' modern conditions best) would have encouraged a line of argument for strengthening this institution and helping it to perform its functions adequately. The argument for providing the nuclear family with the resources necessary for its adequate functioning (housing, family allowances, financial and social provision for the aged in order to free it from wider kinship entanglements and enable it to concentrate on the task of socialising the young) could receive powerful justification from the theory. But one looks through functionalist literature in vain for an approach of this kind to social policy.[40] More recently, however, the situation seems to have changed. Thus Gouldner tells us that 'in his later writings, Parsons has become increasingly outspoken in his support of governmental regulation of the economy and of some version of the Welfare State in general'.[41] Other functionalists are also said to be moving in this direction partly, it seems, as a belated response to the welfare 'crisis' of the 1960s in the United States.[42] These developments support our

Chapter 5

The Marxist Perspective

Marxism is relevant to welfare on two counts. First, as a comprehensive theory of society it provides an explanation of the nature of welfare and its development in bourgeois and other societies. Secondly, as a normative theory concerned with the transcendence of capitalism it offers a particular view of problems germane to welfare and of their 'definitive' solution. Marxism of course includes Marx's own thought as well as of others whose basic ideas and analyses are close to Marx's. This raises the problem of distinguishing 'Marxist' from a variety of 'radical', 'socialist', 'conflict' or what has been called 'Marxisant' viewpoints. Perhaps the problem can best be approached in terms of the distance from the leading ideas of Marx. This gives us a continuum with some interpretations of welfare closer to Marx's viewpoint than others, although where one draws the line and whom one includes under the rubric of 'Marxist' must remain an arbitrary choice. It is in this sense that I have chosen to focus on the writings of a number of contemporaries, notably Saville, Baran and Sweezy, and Mandel, as examples of Marxist thinking on welfare. But I begin by looking at Marx's own view of welfare.[1]

The Nature of Welfare and its Development

(a) *Karl Marx* Marx's social theory is not directly concerned with the analysis of what we would describe as the institutions of welfare. For one, these institutions – in particular the social services – were scarcely developed in anything like their present form in Marx's lifetime. For another, with the notable exception of factory legislation, Marx paid little attention to the growth of state intervention in Victorian England which in retrospect at least seem to constitute the beginnings of the welfare state. In fact Marx's attitude to capitalism was one of total rejection rather than reform and much of his intellectual effort went into proving that the capitalist system was both unworkable and inhuman. All the same it cannot be denied that the problem of poverty and the degradation of the masses under the regime of unrestrained capitalism and the definitive solution of that problem was at the heart of Marx's moral and intellectual enterprise. Pinker has recently drawn our attention to the 'empiricist' Marx – to the fact that *Capital* abounds in data culled from British blue books on the life and labour of the working people and that knowledge and use of such data remains rare among theorists of Marx's stature.[2] Although much of this data is an indictment of capitalism it also shows Marx's concern for the life-chances of the working people. Moreover, Marx seems unique among major theorists in having examined in some detail a major piece of social legislation, namely, the factory acts. Marx's study of factory legislation is important for several reasons. First, it shows his attitude towards 'reform' – to the possibility of the development of welfare within capitalism. Second, it offers an insight into the Marxian view of the nature of the state in capitalist society, a problem not unrelated to the former. And finally, it offers a 'case-study' – an application by Marx of his social theory to a piece of welfare legislation passed by the capitalist state. But apart from these features of Marx's work – more or less directly relevant to the question of welfare in capitalist society – Marx's theory offers a distinctive view of welfare as well as an explanation of the relation between welfare and society in a broader sense. However, this 'theory of welfare' is far from explicit and has to be constituted from the relevant writings scattered throughout Marx's works.[3]

In essential outlines the Marxian notion of welfare and its relation to different types of society is simple. Marx conceives of welfare as a social (that is, relational) norm based on the values of solidarity and co-operation. In concrete terms, welfare manifests itself in the social recognition of human need and in the organisation of production and distribution in accordance with the criterion of need. But how do the values and norms of welfare relate to different types of social structures in history? To appreciate this relationship we must begin by looking at some of the basic features of Marxian theory briefly.

For Marx the central fact about society is its mode of production – the manner in which its productive activity is organised – which exerts a decisive influence on the structure and processes of society. It includes the forces of production – briefly the technology and other productive resources – and more importantly, the relations of production, i.e. the kind of class or power relationship entailed in the organisation of production. It is Marx's contention that throughout history, in all developed societies including capitalism, this relationship has remained exploitative. To put it very simply, a small minority owns (or controls) the means of production, while the vast majority of the people (the non-owners) are condemned to labour and to live at a subsistence level. The surplus left over and above subsistence is appropriated by the ruling minority by virtue of its effective control (e.g. the nobility and the Church in the Middle Ages) or outright legal ownership (e.g. the capitalists, shareholders) of the means of production, namely land, capital, etc. Much of human history has therefore been characterised by the existence of a small class of the rich and privileged and a vast mass of more or less poor people. However, for Marx the division of society into the ruling and the subject class, the rich and the poor, is not something inevitable or immutable due to, say, human nature. Quite the contrary. For what Marxian theory emphasises above all is the *historical* nature of these categories. For instance, such divisions did not exist in primitive societies nor need they exist in the post-capitalist or socialist society.[4]

Let us follow through this analysis with a brief overview of social evolution. In primitive societies the level of technology is low and the division of labour rudimentary. Hence there is no surplus that could be appropriated by a minority. There is therefore a condition of equality in these societies, an equality at the level of bare subsistence to be sure, but life-chances are more or less equal for all. Thus the terms 'rich' and 'poor' have no meaning in these societies. With advances in technology, the productive powers of society develop

together with the division of labour. An economic surplus over and
above the subsistence level now becomes available. With the ap-
propriation of this surplus by a small minority, the division between
rich and poor arises. In varying degrees and forms this situation of exploitation has existed in all societies – in ancient societies based on
outright slavery, in feudal societies based on serfdom and in modern
bourgeois society on the exploitation of 'free' wage labour. This is how
poverty is created at one pole and riches at the other. Poverty and
wealth are thus little more than the relations of distribution which exist
under any exploitative mode of production. In short the 'causes' of
poverty and riches lie in the mode of production of a society – in the
fundamental economic structure of society itself.[5]

Under the capitalist mode of production the basic structural
elements through which wealth and poverty are generated and
reproduced are: private ownership of the means of production;
production for profit; private property and inheritance; and the allocation of incomes and resources through the market mechanism. For
Marx, these core institutions of capitalism and the underlying values
constitute the very antithesis of a welfare society. Under capitalism incomes and life-chances are distributed almost entirely through the impersonal market mechanism. The dominance of market and cash nexus, according to Marx, denies human needs and social solidarity
altogether. Coercion and competition rather than co-operation and
solidarity lie at the root of capitalist social organisation.[6] For Marx,
then, the values and norms of welfare cannot make much headway in
a society of this type. In particular, for the institutionalisation of
welfare as a central social value, it is necessary that production be
governed by social criteria and distribution by human needs. This in
turn requires that the dominance of the market together with private
ownership of productive resources and production for profit are ended
and communal control established over the conditions of work and living. Marx believed that the conditions for such a transformation are
present within the capitalist society itself. The contradictions of
capitalism result in growing socialist (class) consciousness leading
eventually to a social revolution. With such a revolution capitalism is
transcended (just as feudalism was transcended in an earlier age) and
the foundations of a socialist society – non-exploitative and classless –
are laid. Under socialism, 'need' becomes the central value governing
production and distribution.[7] Marx thus postulates a 'total' concept of

welfare and his vision points to the post-revolutionary society as the true consummation of the principle of welfare. This does not, however, rule out the prospect of reform – of a partial, marginal development of welfare within capitalism itself. Marx believed that largely through the action of the ascendant class – the workers – progressive social institutions could develop within the capitalist society.[8] Just as bourgeois norms and values became partially established within the feudal society and thus began to transform it from within, in the same way socialist values and institutions – among them the social services – can begin to change bourgeois society from within. However, in so far as these developments take place within the bounds of a capitalist society their scope remains limited and they invariably exist in a distorted and contradictory form. Marx therefore remains sceptical about the real nature of such institutions of welfare and the extent to which they can develop within the capitalist society.[9]

In a more concrete form, however, Marx's attitude to social reform can be gauged from his analysis of factory legislation. Marx paid a good deal of attention to the factory acts passed in England and saw them as significant in modifying the capitalist social system.[10] In so far as this early social legislation imposed a limit on exploitation by restricting the hours of work, it recognised the worker as a human being and checked the freedom of the capitalist to exploit under the rules of the market place. For Marx, factory legislation was the first fruit of workers' concerted action against the inhuman conditions of life and labour under capitalism.[11] True, other social groups and classes had also supported factory legislation and in particular the landed aristocracy had helped a great deal with the passage of the legislation (since factory acts could not hurt the landed interests in any way). But for Marx, the mainspring of progress was working-class action and factory legislation was 'the victory of a principle', of the 'political economy of the working class' over the 'political economy of the middle class'.[12] In short, Marx recognises that workers need not wait 'with folded arms' for the day of revolution but could begin to establish socialist values and institutions, piecemeal, within the bourgeois society. This, for Marx, was the main significance of social legislation such as the factory act.

But does the idea of piecemeal social change square with Marx's view of the state? According to Marx's theory, the state in capitalist (or any other class-divided) society largely serves the interest of the

dominant class.[13] Its main purpose within the social formation is to
reproduce the class relations – to maintain and strengthen the given
mode of production, and hence also the existing mode of distribution.
In short, the state is there to maintain the integrity of the system – the
dominant values and social relations entailed in a given mode of
production. However, at the same time Marx recognised the dual
nature of the state in a class society. Thus, while the bourgeois state
remains the stronghold of the propertied classes in general and of
owners of capital in particular, it has to act to some extent as the
representative of the community as a whole. For Marx, herein lies the
essentially contradictory nature of the state in a class society. On the
one hand it represents the community, acts on its behalf and responds
to pressure exerted by various sections of the community. On the
other hand, it remains firmly rooted in the class structure and
therefore, in the long run, cannot act effectively against the interests of
the dominant class whose power and influence remain decisive. Marx
spelled out these contradictions in respect of factory legislation, in that
on the one hand parliament accepted the principle of social regulation
of the capitalist enterprise and on the other hand did very little to see
that the regulations were enforced.[14] Indeed, Marx was tireless in
exposing the limitations of bourgeois reformism, for example the
reluctance of the government to move in these matters, the limitations
of the various measures that reached the statute book, the stubborn
resistance offered and the various means adopted by vested interests
to circumvent the effect of legislation.[15] And lastly, Marx emphasised
the ways in which the core values and institutions of capitalism
frustrated reform. Attempts at effective social regulation continually
came up against the basic ground rules of capitalism – freedom of
enterprise, of buying and selling, the rights of private property and the
like.

Thus to some extent the ambiguity – or rather the duality – in
Marx's thinking about the nature of the bourgeois state and the
prospects of reform sprang from the ambiguous social reality of
mid-Victorian capitalism itself. However, on the whole, Marx's system
determinism – the view that the mode of production determines the
rest of the social structure and that political and administrative intervention can not therefore decisively shape the reality of the
economic order – led him to emphasise the immense difficulty that lay
in the way of reform. This was particularly the case as regards the

poor laws, public health and housing.[16] Marx paid only brief attention to these and attached no significance to the growth of publicly provided education.[17] On the whole, he used the evidence on these issues as an indictment of capitalism and in denying the plausibility of reform. There is, clearly, a contradiction here in Marx's thought of which he does not seem to be aware. If reform had succeeded in one sphere of bourgeois society, namely factory work, the very heart of capitalist production and the accumulation of surplus value, why should it not succeed at least equally well in others, in dealing with poverty and unemployment, health and housing? Marx's writings do not provide an answer to this apparent inconsistency in his view of social change in capitalist society. In fact Marx works with two different models of capitalism, one 'static' and the other 'dynamic'. The former is a tight 'system' model which rules out piecemeal change, while the latter – employed in the case of factory legislation – is a developmental model which allows for change through the action of the workers and through the very 'logic' of the system itself. However, since the first model (where change can only be revolutionary) remains the dominant one, Marx's theory minimises the possibility of certain forms of change – notably the development of the welfare state – in bourgeois society.

To sum up, the main features of the Marxian perspective on welfare are as follows:

1. Welfare entails the regulation of work and living conditions and the distribution of societal resources on the basis of human need.

2. As a social system capitalism is antithetical to welfare.

3. Welfare can begin to be established partially in capitalist society through collective action on the part of the workers. However, given the nature of the capitalist social system, the prospects for reform remain meagre.

4. In a class-divided society, the government and the state apparatus largely serves the interest of the dominant class. But the universality of the state requires it to act, to some extent, on behalf of the community as a whole. Hence the bourgeois state is Janus-faced as regards welfare. Social measures may be accepted in form but not realised in substance.

5. Welfare can be established fully as a regulative and distributive norm only after the means of production have been socialised and the market-private property system abolished.

Such, in brief outline, is the Marxian view of welfare. Since Marx's time, however, capitalist society has undergone many changes, not least of which is the vastly enlarged role of the state. Has Marxist thought come to terms with these developments? And in what way? For an answer to these questions we turn to contemporary Marxist thinking relevant to welfare.

(b) The Marxists In Marxist literature there is little systematic (not to say detailed) discussion of the nature and significance of the welfare state, while non-statutory forms of welfare are rarely mentioned. Much of the relevant discussion of welfare thus tends to be indirect – a by-product of the thinking about such questions as changes in the capitalist economy, the nature and role of the state in bourgeois society, the class structure of advanced capitalism and the like, rather than about social services as such.[18]

Marx's own model of capitalism was largely of the classical *laissez-faire* variety. Since then the social services have expanded greatly as has the role of the government generally in the economic and social life of Western countries. Marxists therefore have to come to grips with this new development; they have to explain the causes and consequences of increased state intervention including that form of intervention known as the welfare state. The Marxist contribution on this subject has largely taken the form of a polemic against the social democratic view of the welfare state. These views may be summarised as follows: that the welfare state is largely a product of the socialist movement, in particular of socialist governments; that from the standpoint of security and equality it has meant a significant modification of capitalism; and that it is a 'part-way' if not a 'half-way' house to socialism. In general Marxist analysis has been concerned with denying these propositions. The argument put forward is that neither the origins nor the consequences of the welfare state are socialist in nature. Saville,[19] for example, sees the development of the welfare state as a result of the interaction of three main factors: the struggle of the working class against their exploitation; the requirements of industrial capitalism for a more efficient environment in which to operate – in particular the need for a highly productive labour force; and the recognition by the propertied classes of the price that has to be paid for political security (the famous 'ransom' of Joseph Chamberlain). As a Marxist, Saville stresses the role of the working class and of the labour movement in bringing about this

change but warns that 'it would be historically incorrect and politically an error to under-estimate the importance of either of the other
(two) factors. . . . To do so would be to accept the illusion that changes
are of greater significance than in fact they are, as well as to misread
the essential character of contemporary capitalism.'[20] Saville points
out that in nineteenth-century Britain, social reform and welfare
was largely the concern of the middle classes and the case for positive
social policies was often argued on grounds of social and economic
efficiency and political stability. In the twentieth century the context of
the argument has changed radically. For example, the emergence of
the labour movement and of the socialist alternative has vastly changed the meaning of what threatens the stability of society. But concern
with stability and efficiency has played an important part in the enact-
ment of various social measures in this century.[21]

Domhoff makes a similar point in the American context.[22] He
draws attention to upper- and middle-class ascendancy (in respect of
initiation, financing and control) over various pressure groups and
research organisations that spearheaded the campaign for social
legislation and reform.[23] As in Britain, the themes uppermost in the
minds of the reformers were the containment of labour unrest and
political instability through moderate reforms and the attainment of
greater rationality and efficiency in industry. Significantly enough,
if there was one group that played hardly any part in the passage of
early social security legislation in the United States, it was organised
labour. Thus Domhoff shows that workmen's compensation, aimed
primarily at eliminating lengthy and potentially costly litigation, was
'forced upon organised labour by moderate members of the power
elite'.[24]

As regards the claim of egalitarian consequences, Marxist writers
have no difficulty in showing that the social services are largely financed by the working classes and that the redistribution involved is, in the
main, horizontal (within classes) rather than vertical (between
classes).[25] Thus Saville concludes that the 'welfare state is the twentieth
century version of the Victorian ideal of self-help . . . the state now
"saves" for the working class and translates the savings into social
services'.[26] Domhoff writes in a similar vein on the social security
legislation of the New Deal. 'The masses, in short, were being forced
to save part of their incomes for a rainy day.'[27] The distribution of
income, status and power, in a word the class structure, was virtually

unaffected by the social security legislation of the New Deal. The 'wealth distribution did not change, decision-making power remained in the hands of upper class leaders, and the basic principles that encased the conflict were set forth by moderate members of the power elite'.[28] The expansion of social services and increased taxation since the early years of this century, notes Saville, has made little difference to the distribution of wealth in Britain which remains highly unequal.[29] And while income distribution 'has proved more amenable to political pressure from the Labour movement, there exists within any capitalist society strong and powerful tendencies offsetting egalitarian measures'.[30])

Saville focuses his attention on Britain but his arguments (and those of Domhoff) apply more generally to the relation between capitalist society and the welfare state. Stated very briefly and put in language somewhat different from Saville's this relationship has to do with (a) system integration or the integration of functions and institutions and (b) social integration and social control or the integration of social classes and groups and the maintenance of order. Let us look at each of these briefly. The first refers to (the various measures necessary for the continuation, stability and efficient working of the capitalist industrial system. For example, state-provided education, much of public health and environmental measures of the type enacted in nineteenth-century Britain, the New Deal in the United States – a Keynesian measure for bolstering up the economy – are forms of state intervention aimed at stability and/or efficient functioning of capitalism. Here the Marxist stress on changes in the nature of capitalist economy – from competitive and entrepreneurial to corporate and monopolistic – is important. Mandel,[31] for example, argues that the scale and capital-intensive operations of large corporations require stability – of consumption as well as investment. To ensure this, state intervention in economic life becomes necessary and the 'systems of social insurance, social security, unemployment pay, etc.' form a part of such stabilisers.[32] Mandel employs a similar line of reasoning with regard to the development of health and educational services, namely, that these measures are motivated by the desire to increase productivity and the productive life of the worker.[33] While a fuller discussion and critique of the Marxist position must be reserved for a later section of this chapter, the blatantly 'functionalist' nature of the argument – especially evident in Mandel – is worth noting. True, as a historian, Saville is far more aware of the 'actors' (that is, social groups and classes) involved in the development of the social services; for example, he speaks of the struggle of the working class against exploitation as one of the contributory factors. But(on the whole there is a (quite understandable) tendency among Marxists, to ascribe the development of the welfare state largely to the functional necessities of capitalism.)

System integration is also the(theme of Baran and Sweezy.[34] State intervention, according to these writers, tends to increase in conditions of advanced capitalism for reasons inherent in the nature of the system itself. Thus, since the productive potential of capitalism continually outstrips the market for its product, the government increasingly tends to underwrite business activity.[35] Baran and Sweezy, in common with other Marxists, warn against the error of equating capitalism with *laissez-faire* and minimal government. This is an error into which those brought up on the history and traditions of Anglo-American societies are more likely to fall. Since capitalism in these societies began with a strong tradition of individualism and *laissez-faire*, increasing state intervention in welfare and state collectivism generally tend to be seen as the decline of capitalism and even as a development towards socialism. As Mandel puts it, 'the doctrine of *laissez-faire* is only a stage in the development of bourgeois ideology; it has meaning only for a particular phase of capitalism and for a quite limited geographical area'.[36] Mandel, as well as Miliband [37] and others, draws attention to the state-collectivism of Nazi Germany, to the mercantilist state of pre-industrial Europe and to the active role of the state in promoting capitalist economic development in Germany and Japan, for example. While the concrete objectives of state intervention in early and advanced capitalist societies differ, what is common is that the result is not the abolition but 'the strengthening of the wealth and power of the bourgeoisie'.[38])

Social integration, or more appropriately(social control, the other main function of the bourgeois welfare state has to do with the maintenance of order and the reduction of social conflict and tension.[39] From the viewpoint of the ruling classes this often means reducing the workers' hostility towards the capitalist regime, winning them over to the 'national' cause, and building a 'national' identity and purpose so that class conflict is emasculated. Bismarck's Germany provides a good example of a social policy of this kind.[40] (Bismarck's policy of social insurance had wide repercussions – it was emulated by many continental countries, it encouraged interventionist thinking in the United States and served as a model for Lloyd George's social reform.) The Marxist view of welfare as social control conjures up a 'conspiracy' theory of social development. With Bismarck's social policy, which may be said to mark the beginning of the welfare state in the Western world, the 'conspiracy' was all too evident. Bismarck's avowed aim was to crush revolutionary socialism – a growing political force in Germany – and to win over the German workers behind his policy of state paternalism. Bismarck followed up his repressive anti-socialist measures with the announcement of a comprehensive programme of social insurance.[41] His aims in launching state welfare were openly and unashamedly expedient. In other countries, the objectives were not so obvious. None the less, towards the close of the nineteenth century, as imperial rivalry between the major European nation-states sharpened and the threat of radical socialism seemed to grow, the ruling classes everywhere attempted to 'nationalise' the lower classes – to 'incorporate' the workers into the bourgeois social order – through social reform. Thus Miliband quotes Balfour, Tory prime minister at the beginning of this century, 'social legislation . . . is not merely to be distinguished from Socialist legislation, but is its most direct opposite and its most effective antidote'.[42]

Not only in Germany and Italy but in Britain too there were important links between an imperial posture abroad and the plan for social reform at home.[43] The question of narrowing the gulf between the classes and thereby securing national cohesion was one that exercised statesmen a great deal at the turn of the century. But imperial rivalry and the possibility of war also raised the question of 'national efficiency' in an acute form.[44] Standards of health and education in *laissez-faire* Britain contrasted unfavourably with the social efficiency of a collectivist Germany (and in a somewhat different form with that of Japan). Meanwhile the changed economic and political circumstances in which Britain found herself – no longer the 'workshop of the world' and faced with intense economic and military competition – were paralleled by changes in ideology. Thus Spencerian evolutionism, which came down heavily in favour of *laissez-faire*, was overshadowed by an altogether different current of evolutionary thought.[45] In this new Social Darwinism of Benjamin Kidd, Karl Pearson and others, survival of the fittest referred no longer to the individual but to the

group – the race, the nation, the species. No nation could hope to survive in the coming struggle for existence, taught this new doctrine, unless it improved its racial stock physically and mentally and breached
those deep cleavages within its body politic which set one class apart
from the other. In short, the demands of imperialism abroad and the
threat of an internationally-minded socialism at home were making
laissez-faire untenable in countries like Britain. The twin demands of
efficiency and social harmony were changing capitalism, at least in the
Old World, from a *laissez-faire* to an interventionist system.

The Marxist position may thus be summarised as one that sees the
development of state welfare as a bourgeois response to the threat of
radical socialism – in an age of imperial rivalry and corporate
capitalism – and as a form of rationalisation and bureaucratisation of
capitalism (greater efficiency, order and predictability). *Laissez-faire*
policy is thus abandoned but the resulting changes do not significantly
alter the position of the working class – in terms of the distribution of
power and privilege – within the structure of capitalism.

The contemporary Marxist position on welfare seems to differ from
Marx's chiefly in one respect. In measures such as factory legislation
Marx saw a significant modification of capitalism (communal control
over working conditions, restrictions on capitalists' freedom to exploit,
improvements in workers' life-chances) brought about largely through
working-class action and showing a way for the gradual transformation of capitalism from within. Contemporary Marxists no longer see
such interventionism as a triumph of the 'political economy of the
working-class over that of the middle class'. Such piecemeal changes
are rather seen as beneficial, if not necessary 'adjustments' to
capitalism often initiated by sections of the ruling classes themselves.
The role of the working class in exerting pressure for change is not
denied but in its overall effect the welfare state is seen as a 'logical' extension and consolidation of capitalism rather than its negation. Marx
with his revolutionary optimism did not seriously brook the prospect
of the 'incorporation' of the working class, but the political problem
facing the Marxists is precisely that of working-class accommodation
to bourgeois society. The welfare state has clearly helped in this accommodation (as well as being an expression of it) at only a small
price to the bourgeoisie, for it has not involved any substantial altera-
tion in the class character of income and wealth distribution. There is
ample evidence on which Marxists can draw to show that social

reform has not even succeeded in eliminating poverty. In fact the logic of Marxist argument (in line with the system determinism of Marx) is that 'problems' such as poverty and inequality of incomes are an integral part of the capitalist system and cannot be solved within the framework of capitalism. As Mandel for example argues, first, any attempt at a substantial class transfer of incomes is likely to meet the 'fierce resistance' of the privileged. Second, and more important, the long-term effect of a real rise in subsistence wage (abolition of poverty) would be disastrous for the capitalist economy. For a real redistribution of income – a substantial rise in wages without a rise in productivity – will make a serious inroad into profits, the pivot on which the capitalist economy turns.[46] In a word, capitalism cannot accommodate the elimination of poverty. For Mandel, then, the welfare state is essentially a device for social control and not a system of income redistribution. 'It is obvious that what we have here is a measure with political and social aims, a lubrication of the social mechanism intended to avoid an explosion, and not an economic evolution which in some way or other, contradicts the relative impoverishment of the proletariat.'[47]

It would be wrong, however, to convey the impression that there is no more to Marxist thinking on the subject than a systems (functionalist) analysis of the relation between the part (welfare) and the whole (capitalism). At least some Marxists, Baran and Sweezy, for example, also analyse welfare policy in terms of a conflict of values and interests. Thus Baran and Sweezy are much less inclined to see the welfare state as simply a handmaiden of monopoly capitalism. True, the New Deal which inaugurated the state social security programme in the United States was largely aimed at system integration and social control. But these writers also point out the limitations, indeed the failure, of the New Deal as a counter-cyclical measure. This failure was due mainly to the limited scope of state intervention – of transfer payments and government spending – under the programme. It was the war rather than the New Deal that eventually pulled the United States and indeed world capitalism out of the depression. The New Deal was hamstrung because 'given the power structure of United States monopoly capitalism, the increase of civilian spending had about reached its outer limits by 1939. The forces opposing further expansion were too strong to overcome.'[48] Baran and Sweezy offer no details of these opposing forces but give two examples of such vested interests from the post-war years: real estate interests opposed to public housing and the medical profession opposed to publicly provided medical care. In these two cases, state schemes were opposed bitterly and never allowed to materialise since they would undercut private enterprise.[49] However, civilian state spending also faces opposition, for example in the case of public education, simply because it threatens the existing structure of privileges. Baran and Sweezy underline their argument by contrasting arms expenditure – a form of public spending and pump priming operation readily acceptable to the most powerful and influential groups in American society – with expenditure on the social services. While both may serve equally well as a way of maintaining demand and sustaining a high level of economic activity, in other respects they have very different consequences. The welfare state is far more likely to benefit the masses than the welfare state and Baran and Sweezy remain sceptical about the extent to which social services can develop in the United States.[50] Baran and Sweezy, then, are far less inclined to equate advanced capitalism with the welfare state. Social services are not simply a 'functional necessity' of corporate capitalism. Functional relationships are undoubtedly involved but there are alternatives, e.g. between warfare and welfare type state expenditure, and these, in turn, relate to conflicting values and interests. For Mandel, on the other hand, the distinction between the 'warfare' and 'welfare' state is not so basic. Nazi Germany was the classic combination of a fascist (war) economy with a highly developed welfare state. Fascism (repression) and the welfare state (reform) remain two possible responses on the part of the ruling class to the basic economic contradictions of capitalism.[51]

To summarise: the *Marxist* position seems to differ from the *Marxian* largely in emphasis. The Marxists see the change from *laissez-faire* to interventionist capitalism primarily in terms of a 'functional' rather than a 'dialectical' logic of capitalist development. The emphasis is on the 'hard' model in Marx – the synchronic, unchanging system maintaining aspects of capitalism – which rules out the possibility of significant piecemeal changes. Nowadays Marx's evolutionary model of socialism, which sees change as cumulative and leading to a transformation of the old order through the action of the working class, is more likely to be evoked by social democrats (without mentioning Marx of course) in support of welfare state policies. Earlier I have tried to summarise Marx's view of welfare (see. p. 67). Three additional points need to be made to take the view of contemporary Marxists into account and thus complement the earlier summary (points 1–5). These are as follows:

6. Social services make important contributions to the efficient and smooth working of the capitalist economy.
7. They help to mitigate class conflict and thus stabilise the social order.
8. Not surprisingly, therefore, the initiative for the development of social services often comes from sections of the ruling class itself.

These points together with the summary presented earlier thus provide a brief outline of the Marxist perspective on welfare. This summary outline will be used as a reference point in the discussion that follows.

The Marxist Perspective: An Assessment

(a) The Concept of Welfare The idea of 'need' and of a society (a mode of production) founded on the basis of the satisfaction of human needs is central to Marxist thought. Indeed a basic concern of Marx's sociology may be said to find an answer to the question – how is a society possible in which the conditions of life and labour in the broadest sense are regulated in accordance with human needs? Need-based distribution of resources is only one aspect of this need-centred society. Thus the Marxian concept is focused on the welfare society rather than on the institution of welfare as such. Perhaps the best way of looking at this view of welfare is to compare it with the approach of social administration discussed earlier (see chapter 1). First, there is no basic difference between the Marxist notion of welfare and that of social administration – both consider the idea of meeting needs as central to welfare. In this Marxism and social administration differ from the other approaches discussed above, none of which focuses on need. In the citizenship view the social services appear as a part of the idea of citizenship rights in modern society; in the functionalist approach they appear as integrative institutions and are seen in terms of the contribution they make to the functioning of society. By contrast the

Marxist definition of welfare (as indeed that of social administration) focuses on a particular value or principle (need) as a basis of social organisation and on its progressive realisation in society. If there is a difference between the two, it is one of degree rather than of kind. The Marxist view of social policy is much wider than that of social administration. Marxism refuses to equate social policy with a specific range and level of needs (i.e. concerning education, health, housing and subsistence income) confined to a limited area of need-based distribution as supplementary to the dominant market system. Thus one could say that the Marxist commitment to welfare is more thoroughgoing, more 'total'. It takes its stand more on principle (that need should be the basic distributive principle) than on a pragmatic (administrative) view of what has come to be seen as the legitimate concern of the social services.

Now the interesting point is that over the years social administration itself has been extending the frontiers of what is defined as 'social policy'. In a seminal paper published some twenty years ago Titmuss argued that the conception of social policy must include occupational and fiscal provision besides the social services.[52] Later Titmuss's studies of income distribution helped to place the debate about social services in that wider setting.[53] More recently, Pinker has raised the question whether public utilities such as transport should be included in the definition of services relevant to social policy.[54] Townsend has also argued in favour of a broad conception of social policy.[55] In short, we are beginning to see a wider view of policy, a development which brings social administration closer to the Marxist approach. The focus is tending to be less on the administration of particular services and somewhat more on the basic principles of distribution, and their implication for the supply of different goods and services and for the relationship between various groups and individuals. Indeed looking further back at the controversy over the definition of social policy we can see that at the turn of the century the Webbs were fighting for a broader definition of social policy – for extending the area of social intervention – against those who wished to keep social policy within the bounds of the Poor Law.[56] Titmuss's approach should be seen as continuing this tradition of questioning the somewhat narrow, administrative, definition of policy and breaking down those barriers which help to keep social policy within a carefully defined administrative context. The Marxist concept of welfare of course encompasses those of Titmuss and the Webbs but goes further. Perhaps it can best be seen as an ideal-type, a theoretical limiting case: a welfare society is one where the social organisation in general and the distribution of goods and services in particular is entirely need-based. Its opposite, the 'diswelfare' society is one where needs are entirely disregarded and the market reigns supreme. Both are ideal-types. In actual terms, the systems are bound to be mixed. This polarisation helps us to see social policy as a continuum at one end of which is what I have elsewhere called a 'normative' social policy [57] ('to each according to his needs') and at the other the 'residual' (entirely market-based) with the 'institutional' (mixed system) somewhere in the middle.

A second characteristic of the Marxist notion of welfare (which it once again shares with social administration) is that it is relatively simple and empirically-based. The development of welfare is largely a question of a higher proportion of goods and services (or money income) being distributed on the basis of need. It may be somewhat misleading to attribute such a crude 'materialist' view of social policy to Marxism (and especially to social administration) for clearly other criteria, such as democratic administration, freedom and the dignity of the individual, are also involved. None the less this quantitative approach, which seems basic to both Marxism and social administration, is less ambiguous than other approaches which link up social policy with the far more elusive notions of citizenship or integration.

Thirdly, and once again in common with social administration, Marxism focuses on the satisfaction of individual needs. The Marxist notion of 'to each according to his needs' does not refer to the 'needs' of society (as in functionalist analysis) but to those of the individual. Thus at least from this viewpoint Marxism shares a perspective with social administration that is humanistic and has the advantage of clarity and empirical reference. This is not to deny that as a guide to policy-making the concept of need remains highly problematic. Who is to decide what the needs in any given case are? Is it to be a political, administrative or professional decision? And what part does the individual himself play in defining need? Furthermore, even in those higher reaches of communism where the market will disappear altogether, resources would presumably still remain scarce in relation to 'needs'. How are priorities to be decided in such a social system and how would one evaluate policies? These are thorny questions to which neither Marx himself nor the Marxists seem to have an answer. However, any definition of social policy which centres on needs and their fulfilment must grapple with these issues and we cannot say that social administration has done very much better. This is one area, however, where social administration may be in a position to contribute to the problems of applied Marxism. At any rate it is a terrain on which Marxists (serious ones, that is) and social administration could engage in a fruitful dialogue.

Finally we must draw attention to one of the limitations of the Marxist view of welfare. Unlike functionalism, it does not offer a way of conceptualising systems of welfare other than the social services, for example religious and charitable assistance, enterprise welfare and mutual aid. For this there are several reasons. First, the object of study for the Marxist is the mode of production, the basic economic structure of society, and his focus tends to be on the society-state level. Secondly, as a normative theory Marxism is concerned with nothing less than total transformation of society. These characteristics – a highly generalised approach and a commitment to fundamental change – are not conducive to the study of the institution of welfare *per se*. Thirdly, conflict and change rather than community and integration tend to be the basic focus of Marxism (at least in respect of capitalist and other class societies). This too inhibits the conceptualisation of 'welfare' as a component of different collectivities – of which the society is only one.

(b) The Development of Welfare in Capitalist Society We have seen that Marx was sceptical about the extent to which social services and other cognate measures (such as factory legislation), which take need into consideration, could become established in bourgeois society. A major reason for this was his belief that the values and institutions of welfare are incompatible with the basic structure of capitalism. He therefore looked towards the supersession of capitalism for the foundation of a welfare society. The substantial expansion of social services and state intervention generally since Marx's time have left little doubt about the extent to which the distribution of resources can be collectivised within the framework of capitalism. Marx's followers have tried to explain this change in terms of the positive functions of social services for capitalism. There is little doubt, however, that in retrospect Marxist thinking seems overly deterministic. That basic capitalist values and institutions can accommodate a good deal of

state intervention and collectivist social policies seems not to have been anticipated by pre-war Marxist theory. Hence, in part, the confusion about the nature of post-war welfare capitalism.

This discrepancy between theory and evidence calls into question the validity of the Marxist 'system' model of society. For the Marxist, the social system of capitalism (as indeed of any other mode of production) is a tightly inter-related whole. In this system, the economic 'base' is the decisive element which dominates the 'super-structures' such as politics, law, ideology, etc. Hence, for the Marxist, legislation – political and administrative measures – cannot effectively change the economic (e.g. distributive) relationships which are rooted in the mode of production. Clearly, a century of social change since Marx's time underlines the over-deterministic nature of his model. A great deal of change has been brought about through democratic political institutions. However, more recent evidence points the other way. For what the history of post-war reforms, at any rate in Britain and the United States, shows above all is the difficulty of establishing the values and institutions of public welfare even partially in a society whose 'core' institutions remain capitalist.[58] A variety of influences, direct and indirect, stemming from the market system and from the established class structure reassert themselves in the wake of reform eroding the welfare state. The influence of the 'system' is nowhere clearer than in the way in which income and wealth distribution remains relatively immune from the effects of taxation.[59] Finally, the way in which the social services and other forms of welfare operating within a highly stratified social order can benefit the upper and middle classes has been amply demonstrated by recent social research.[60] In sum, the guiding principle of the Marxist approach, namely that the institution of welfare (or indeed any other social institution) must be looked at in relation to the system as a whole, cannot be faulted. Nor can we disregard the influence of the 'core' economic (e.g. the market) and social (e.g. class) institutions on the nature and development of welfare. Indeed any serious analysis of social policy and the strategy of social change must face up to these major insights of Marxist theory. What is open to question, however, is the *degree* of system determinism suggested by Marxists. And it is this relative autonomy of politics, of the state in relation to the economic structure – an autonomy whose limits cannot be laid down by any theory – that causes the 'trouble'. It is this 'freedom' which is the source of hope, as indeed of despair, for the social reformer in capitalist society. At any rate Marxist determinism is a useful corrective to the over-optimistic liberal assumption, so widely prevalent in the years after the 1939–45 war, that a democratic state and legislature can modify the basic economic structure of society and transform capitalist society once and for all into a welfare state.

(We turn next to the role of the working class in the development of welfare in capitalist society. Marx himself considered working-class action as decisive in the process, for example in the development of factory legislation. Contemporary Marxists with the advantage of hindsight stress the part played by other social groups and classes, even if at times in response to working-class pressure for change. Besides, contemporary Marxists recognise other reasons for the growth of state intervention.)These have largely to do with 'system integration', educational services being a prime example. It is important to note here a difference between Marx's own explanation of the development of social policy which is usually in terms of group action (by workers, capitalists, etc.) and those of contemporary Marxists which is largely in functionalist terms ('needs' of the capitalist system). The weaknesses of the latter explanation are many. First, it has a tendency to confound the question of the origins of social institutions with their consequences [61] and, in effect, explain the former by the latter. As we have seen earlier (see chapter 4) any social measure has a number of consequences. To emphasise only one of these and single it out as the 'cause' is arbitrary; other consequences can equally claim the status of a cause. Secondly, this type of explanation can be seriously misleading in that it ignores the vital distinction between intended and unintended consequence of action. Thirdly, a satisfactory explanation must bring into the analysis some account of the values and group interests involved and the sort of action taken by the key protagonists which led to change. Marx offers such an account of the development of factory legislation, and however we may disagree with his interpretation his approach is illuminating. Contemporary Marxists have tended to abandon the group-action perspective in favour of a functionalist analysis. This is to be regretted for one of the strengths of the Marxist approach over functionalism is that it combines a 'system' analysis (society as an interconnected whole) with a group perspective (social change resulting from conflict of values and interests). Again it is this combination of perspectives that is lacking in

social administration where some of the best studies of the development of social policy make use of a group-action perspective but lack
an overall conception of social structure within which particular accounts of development could be meaningfully located.[62] The result is a
very much open-ended *ad hoc* analysis which does not enable us to
make sense of the dialectic between society and social policy as a
whole.

Coming back, however, to the question of working-class action,
evidence certainly supports the thesis of the influence of organised
workers on welfare. Thus it is hardly a coincidence that the two
Western industrial countries where state welfare is least developed are
also countries where, for various reasons, trade unionism has been
slow to develop.[63] Directly or indirectly, then, the pressure of the
organised working class remains important although clearly, action by
other classes and groups is also involved, as Marx himself noted in the
case of factory legislation. There is little doubt, however, that in its
preoccupation with the two major classes in capitalist society, Marxist
analysis tends to ignore the influence of other important, if subsidiary,
social groupings, e.g. the professionals. Moreover, in stressing
economic interest as the mainspring of action, Marxists take little
notice of ideologies and beliefs as an independent influence on social
development. Thus the role cf philanthropy and humanitarian values,
of professional and bureaucratic 'rationality' (somewhat different from
market 'rationality' and the 'logic' of corporate capitalism) tends to be
omitted from Marxist accounts of social policy.[64] It must be
remembered however that no theory can provide an exhaustive account (nor is it meant to) of a social phenomenon. It has to select and
focus on what is of major importance. And here there can be little
doubt that working-class action is a far more potent explanation of the
development of the welfare state than, say, the influence of
philanthropy or the professions. This is not to deny that in the case of
some social services – child-care, the treatment of the mentally ill or
environmental health, for example – philanthropic or professional influence may have been paramount. What is necessary however is to
think in terms of a hierarchy of influences, i.e. to assign 'weight' to the
factors involved. Here again the Marxist approach, based on a
theoretical view of the social structure, is a useful corrective to the
descriptive, often historical accounts of social policy prevalent in
social administration. For it is not very helpful to simply list say half-

a-dozen 'factors' which might include personalities (the Webbs), social research (poverty studies of Booth and Rowntree), wide-ranging pressure groups (from small humanitarian organisations to the labour movement), without any attempt to indicate which are the more important, general and enduring influences. In short, there is a need to link the type and level of social policy development with particular explanatory factors[65] and also to forge stronger links between these 'factors' and the social structure.

(c) Implications for policy As we have mentioned earlier (see chapter 4) the practical implications of a social theory are hard to specify. The difficulty is, if anything, greater with Marxism, a theory pitched at a high level of generality and rich in ambiguity. At any rate the preceding discussion would have already suggested some of the policy implications of the Marxist view of society. Let us try and focus on what seem to be some of the more important consequences of holding such a view.

First Marxists concede that social reform and further development of comprehensive social services remains feasible in capitalist society. What they hold as utopian or illusory is the view that such reforms can weaken capitalism or modify the class structure in any significant manner. In other words the state, by pooling the nation's resources (the insurance principle in a wider sense), can provide services which afford a good deal of security and improved life-chances to the individual without altering the structure of inequality between classes appreciably. Marxist theory therefore offers cold comfort to those who see social policy as a means of achieving substantial class equality within the framework of a capitalist society.

Second, Marxist theory suggests the need for constant struggle on the part of the working class to maintain the welfare state. In so far as the social services represent concessions won from capital they are likely to be whittled away unless fought for regularly. For the Marxist there is no social policy that can solve problems such as poverty once and for all in capitalist society. Rather the situation is more akin to a see-sawing battle. The social wage as much as the market wage is a part of the ongoing conflict of class interests and values.

Third, since the welfare state does not change the class relations and the economic structure of capitalism significantly, social reformism does not seem to rank high in the Marxist scheme of values. Indeed in so far as the welfare state helps in the 'incorporation' of workers by making capitalism more stable, efficient and humane it hinders rather than helps the cause of revolution. In principle, Marxists do emphasise the link between piecemeal reform and the struggle for fundamental change.[66] But in practice the commitment to a revolutionary overthrow of the existing social order weakens Marxist commitment to welfare. At best the latter tends to be seen as a means to the former, which remains the Marxist's primary commitment. Moreover, the awareness that social reforms have a negative feedback as far as revolutionary ardour is concerned is likely to weaken the struggle for welfare further. True, we have argued that the Marxist notion of welfare, centred on need, is intrinsically humanitarian. But this is so only in an ultimate sense, that is under conditions of socialism. Meanwhile the commitment is to the overthrow of the system, to the revolution. Now Marx was able to combine a measure of humanitarianism and compassion with revolutionary commitment. He wrote eloquently of the way in which factory acts had improved the life-chances of the working people. Contemporary Marxists, however, show little of this humanism. In contemporary Marxist discussion of the social services, the stress is almost entirely on their relationship with the capitalist system and rarely on the benefits they might bring to the masses.[67] In short, it seems that neither the normative nor the descriptive elements of Marxist theory lend much support to an ameliorative, humanitarian social policy.

Finally, Marxists' total approach to welfare is inimical to the study of specific problems and the attempt to solve them in a piecemeal fashion. Earlier we argued in favour of a wider social structural perspective on welfare which the Marxist theory provides. Here we must express some reservations. The totalising perspective is useful and liberating – but only when employed in conjunction with the study of a specific area and social practice. Otherwise one might end up by dissolving the identity of specific institutional areas and practices into a highly general, schematised view of social reality. Nothing would be gained and a great deal lost if detailed and painstaking studies of particular aspects of society were to be abandoned in favour of rhetoric and incantation.

Part 2

Social Structure and Welfare

From Theory to Application: a Postscript and a Preface

The preceding chapters have presented five different perspectives on welfare of varying scope and generality. But differing viewpoints are not necessarily conflicting. I hope this has emerged in the course of the discussion. Indeed the fact that they vary in scope and generality means that there is room for complementary as well as symbiotic relationships. However that may be, it is not my intention to attempt a theoretical synthesis. Such a task, even if it is desirable, cannot be attempted here. The main objective of Part One was to present some of the principal sociological arguments regarding the nature and development of welfare. It must be left to students of social policy to decide which of these theoretical resources are of greater validity and use.

However, I am aware that I cannot evade theoretical choice altogether. The second part of the book deals with the nature of welfare in developed societies. It is consequently an interpretation and like all interpretations must entail some form of 'theory'. It is important therefore to declare one's theoretical hand.

Three main ideas have served as a guideline to the explorations that follow. First, that social institutions must be analysed as a part of the wider social system and that the latter is best seen in terms of a distinctive mode of production. We therefore look at welfare in capitalist and socialist societies respectively rather than in industrial society. Second, that welfare must be seen as a social institution and not equated with any one type of social provision. Hence our analysis is not confined to the social services but includes other forms of provision, notably occupational and fiscal benefits. Third, that class and stratification constitutes the most important aspect of the social structure. Hence we focus on the relationship between class and welfare in both capitalist and socialist society. Finally, it should be clear that the approach adopted here is eclectic – it is indebted, above all, to Marx, Titmuss and the functionalists.

Chapter 6

Capitalist Society and Social Welfare

The aim of this chapter is three-fold: to outline the nature of welfare institutions and policies in industrialised capitalist societies; to explain the major similarities and dissimilarities in this regard; and lastly, to point out some of the main consequences of the development of the welfare state. Clearly, to attempt such a task within the confines of a single chapter means that often we can do little more than outline analytical perspectives or make an important point briefly without fuller discussion or documentation. Moreover, since the sociological study of welfare (including cross-national comparison) remains notoriously undeveloped, many of the issues raised and interpretations offered are not based on existing studies and researches. Much of what is said below, especially in the sections on development and consequences of welfare, must therefore be treated as hypotheses – often based solely on British material – that need to be tested against wide-ranging evidence. In other words, a good deal of this chapter should be seen as an exploration rather than an attempt to map out and signpost a well-known terrain.

The Nature of Welfare in Capitalist Society

What is the nature of social welfare institutions in capitalist society? The approach to this question depends on what we believe to be the most significant features of welfare systems. Undoubtedly an important feature of a country's system of welfare is the role of the social services, i.e. the extent of state responsibility for the provision of basic needs. Our discussion will centre around this element. To focus on the scope of the public sector in welfare is, no doubt, to take a somewhat crude and limited view of the subject matter. Welfare systems and policies of capitalist countries vary in a thousand different ways and few of these can be ruled out, *a priori*, as unimportant. However, the ideal way of studying welfare is one thing and what is feasible is quite another. Moreover, we must distinguish between 'macro' and 'micro' levels of study. This book is pitched at the macro level of analysis. It is mainly concerned with the broader features of the relationship between social structure and welfare rather than with detailed comparison of aspects of the social services. It is in this context that the focus on one major element, namely the scope of state provision, seems justified. Finally, it must be remembered that we have argued for a view of social policy that is not restricted to the social services. It would therefore be necessary to look at other forms of welfare as well though, largely due to limitations of data, the review must be brief and tentative.

The main types of arrangements through which needs may be met in capitalist society are the social services, fiscal benefits, occupational welfare, mutual aid and charitable or voluntary assistance. To a greater or lesser extent (and in varying forms) these are to be found in every country. But the mix varies. What determines this mix and how has it changed in the course of the development of capitalist society? The question can usefully be approached in terms of two basic types (or models) of welfare based on the scope of statutory provision. The 'residual' and 'institutional' models are well known as two distinctive approaches to policy[1] (what *should* be done). They can usefully be adapted to depict (what *is*) the nature of welfare arrangements in capitalist society. Let us briefly remind ourselves of the main features of each of these seen as a model or ideal-type (Table 1). In the residual model the scope of state welfare is minimal. The social services (that is, other than Poor Law type of assistance) are largely undeveloped

TABLE 1: Type of Welfare

Main features	Residual	Institutional
1. State responsibility in meeting needs (ideology of state intervention)	Minimal	Optimal
2. Need-based distribution as a value (ideology of distribution)	Marginal	Secondary
3. Range of statutory services (other than the Poor Law)	Limited	Extensive
4. Population covered by statutory services	Minority	Majority
5. Level of benefits	Low	Medium
5a. Proportion of national income spent on state services	Low	Medium
6. Use of means test	Primary	Secondary
7. Nature of clients	Paupers/the Poor	Citizens
8. Status of clients	Low	Medium
9. Orientation of the service	Coercive	Utilitarian
10. Role of non-statutory agencies in welfare	Primary	Secondary

and non-statutory forms of welfare are relatively more prominent. In the second, the position is virtually reversed – the relative weight shifts towards statutory welfare. Taking capitalist societies as a whole we could say that the secular trend has been away from the residual and towards the institutional pattern.[2] Britain provides a good example. Table 2 offers a profile of welfare in Britain in 1860 (early industrial stage) and in 1970. The expansion of state welfare tells its own story. As regards the other forms of welfare, both charity and mutual aid played an important part in meeting needs in early industrial Britain [3] (and in varying degrees in many other capitalist countries, though mutual aid effort seems to have been particularly strong in Britain) [4] but have tended to decline or to be incorporated into state-provided services later.[5] On the other hand at least one non-statutory institution, namely occupational welfare, has developed alongside the expansion of the social services.[6] The growth of occupational welfare, as indeed that of fiscal benefits,[7] must be placed alongside the much

TABLE 2: Welfare in Britain (*c.* 1860 and *c.* 1970)

1. State services	*c. 1860*	*c. 1970*
Income security	None	Old age, invalidity and survivors' pensions; sickness, maternity and work injury and unemployment benefits (virtually universal scheme). Universal family allowances; national assistance
Medical care	None with the exception of lunatic asylums, vaccination and environmental health services	Comprehensive and free health care for the whole population
Education	None with the exception of educational grant (Parliamentary) to religious bodies	Free and compulsory ten-year education; secondary, and higher education with maintenance grants
Housing	None	Over one-quarter of all housing publicly provided, largely at subsidised rent; rent regulation in private sector
	(Poor Law Relief)	
2. Proportion of national income spent on state welfare	1 – 1.5 per cent*	17.4 per cent†
3. Non-statutory welfare	Charitable and mutual aid (friendly societies) predominant	Occupational benefits; charitable and mutual aid prevalent

* Calculated from national income and expenditure data (1861) presented in B.R. Mitchell and Phyllis Deane, *Abstract of British Historical Statistics* (Cambridge University Press, 1962). In 1861 expenditure on the Poor Laws and on Education,

more widely acclaimed development of the social services. Moreover, important changes have also taken place in the sphere of philanthropy. The development of charitable foundations, endowed by, say, Ford or Rockefeller, offers a fascinating example of the way in which the economic and class structures of capitalism interact with the institution of welfare.[8] However the brief survey that follows is restricted to three main forms of welfare: the social services, occupational provision and fiscal benefits.

We begin with the social services. A notable feature here is the policy variation between the major services, namely education, health, income maintenance and housing. Thus education seems to be the one service that is provided along 'institutional' lines everywhere. Countries such as Japan and the United States, which lag behind European countries in respect of state responsibility for income maintenance, health and housing (see below), have long instituted free and compulsory schooling for all.[9] Schooling of about seven to ten years' duration is free and compulsory throughout the advanced capitalist world.[10] Public provision for medical care is also widespread. The United States and Israel are virtually the only countries without a state programme of medical care for the general population.[11] On the other hand, few countries as yet boast a national health service of the British type. Provision is still largely through insurance schemes (as in Britain before the war) which tend to exclude certain groups, for example, very high income earners, from statutory health care.[12] Income maintenance services show rather greater variation. Thus, looking at eight major income security risks we find that in 1967 only fifteen out of twenty industrialised countries offered protection against all eight. The countries without one or more of these schemes were the United States (no sickness and maternity benefits; no family allowance), Japan (no family allowance), Canada (no sickness and maternity benefits), New Zealand (no maternity benefit), Israel (no sickness and unemployment benefits; no invalidity pensions).[13] Cross-national data

---

Art and Science was 1.04 per cent. Data on the expenditure on public health and lunatic asylums are not available but later figures suggest that it could not have exceeded 0.2 per cent of the national income.

† Expenditure on health, education and income security as a percentage of the GNP. Data on health and income security (1966–7) are from *The Cost of Social Security 1964–66* (Geneva: International Labour Office, 1972) and on education from *Statistical Yearbook 1970* (Paris: Unesco, 1971).

on public provision of housing is scarce. But evidence suggests that housing stands at the opposite pole to education; the institutional approach is much less in evidence.[14] In any case, direct state provision of housing is uncommon (Britain, apparently, leads the Western countries in municipal housing)[15] although state assistance towards housing (in one form or another) is fairly widespread among capitalist countries. The range of variation in public provision can perhaps best be illustrated by contrasting Britain and the United States. In the former nearly one-third of all housing is publicly owned; in the latter a mere 2 per cent.[16] State-owned (including local authority) housing is also uncommon in Continental Europe where co-operative, trade-union-sponsored and other forms of non-commercial housing have a substantial share of the total dwellings.[17] The variations in policy in respect of the four major services, referred to briefly above, are important and merit far more attention than they have received in the literature so far. Unfortunately space does not permit further exploration of this issue here.

Although in the large majority of the Western industrialised countries state schemes of welfare are organised more or less along institutional lines, this does not mean that the level of social provision is similar. We have already noted the absence of one or more schemes of income maintenance in several countries. The proportion of population covered and the level of benefits provided under the schemes also vary from one country to another.[18] In short, despite broad similarity of patterns, the scope of state welfare varies widely. This can best be seen by looking at the proportion of G.N.P. spent on the social services. As Table 3 shows, countries vary a good deal in this respect, and as far as can be judged by the level of spending, some are clearly rather more institutional than others. However the comparability of cross-national expenditure data is beset with many problems and these figures must be treated with some scepticism. Moreover, since many factors influence the level of public expenditure on social services, one must be wary of drawing any firm conclusions from these figures. On the other hand, there is little doubt that substantial differences in expenditure reflect, *inter alia*, variations in comprehensiveness of protection, population coverage and adequacy of benefits. It is no coincidence, for example, that both the United States and Japan are among the laggards in social security expenditure while Austria and West Germany are among the leaders.

question as data on non-statutory forms of welfare are scanty. There is little doubt, however, that as far as social security is concerned, occupational welfare acts as an alternative to the social services (for example, medical care insurance in the United States, family allowances in Japan). This is especially the case in Japan where occupational welfare forms a part of the traditional (feudal) paternalistic relation ('familism') between the employee and the employer.[19] Thus it is quite common for the larger Japanese firms to pay family allowances – to non-manual as well as manual workers.[20] The Japanese employer may recognise the needs of his workers in many other ways, e.g. pensions, housing, schooling, kindergarten, hospital and health care, holidays at a beach or a mountain resort, marriage allowance, a loan or financial grant in the event of illness or other family misfortune.[21] Moreover, the 'lifetime' system of employment in Japan (very simply, the employee is expected to join the firm for life and the employer is expected to treat the employee as a permanent member of the firm)[22] differs substantially from the 'rational' labour market policies in Western countries, and acts as a form of unemployment insurance.

Labour relations in the United States are very different from the proto-feudal, collectivist paternalism of Japan. None the less, since the Second World War both pension and medical insurance plans have multiplied at a rapid rate to cover both white-collar and blue-collar workers.[23] And while the relationship between state social security and occupational welfare is far from simple, there is little doubt that in the United States the absence of a public health-care system and the low level of state pensions have encouraged the development of occupational benefits to fill the gap. In Britain the small, flat-rate insurance pension provided under the Beveridge scheme had a similar effect. Helped with tax concessions and other inducements offered by Conservative governments, private occupational pensions have burgeoned.[24] Moreover, it is clear that fringe benefits of various kinds have also been used as a form of income maintenance service for the higher executives and managers against the encroachment of progressive taxation. However, as with the development of state welfare (examined below), many factors have contributed to the growth of occupational welfare. In any case, its development in virtually all advanced capitalist societies suggests that it cannot be considered as an accidental feature – a fortuitous element – of modern welfare. The limited scope of statutory provision, tax concessions and other inducements, the attempt to counteract the effect of taxation on managerial rewards and the like may have accelerated its development. But it would not be an exaggeration to say that like the social services, occupational provision, in one form or another, is an integral part of the welfare systems of advanced capitalist society. The basic reasons for this are to be found in the interaction between industrialism and capitalism. The importance of work, its formal nature and its location in a large-scale bureaucratic setting, the growing importance of labour as a factor of production and hence of 'good' labour relations in promoting efficiency and profitability are among the principal reasons (see p. 37 above).

It is quite clear however that occupational welfare cannot be considered as a 'functional equivalent' of the social services. The crucial difference is that unlike the social services, occupational welfare is essentially a part of the reward structure of the enterprise. This results in substantial inequity between manual and non-manual workers, and more particularly between the former and the managerial and executive groups, in respect of fringe benefits.[25] The social services, on the other hand, do not discriminate along the lines of occupation or similar attributes of status. True, income maintenance services differentiate according to income (e.g. graduated pensions, earnings-related sickness benefits). But this criterion is quite different from one which uses distinctions of rank and occupation to vary the nature of benefits. The former, we would suggest, is a 'quantitative' or 'class' distinction; the latter is more in the nature of a 'qualitative' or 'caste' distinction. Unlike statutory welfare occupational provision is entirely voluntary. Thus a firm may choose not to provide any benefits. Moreover, the nature and amount of occupational benefits would vary between industries and firms, and it is likely that the smaller and less resourceful of these firms, with perhaps a higher proportion of low paid labour, will be the ones with little or no provision.[26] Finally, those outside the labour force (the old, the unemployed) cannot be covered by occupational schemes. Thus occupational welfare may be least helpful where help is most needed. In sum, unless the state were to step in to regulate occupational provision (in which case its independent nature is undermined and it becomes more like state provision), it would tend to replicate and reinforce market determination of life-chances. In Marxist terms we might say that occupational welfare tends to reproduce the capitalist relations of distribution. This can be

seen quite clearly in the case of Japan. The lifetime system of employment and paternalistic welfare provision tends to be limited to the
larger firms. But the majority of the Japanese workers are employed
by the smaller firms [27] and do not therefore enjoy the job security and
fringe benefits typical of the large employers. Furthermore, even in the
large firms there is a substantial pool of 'temporary' employees who
are denied the privileges of permanent tenure and fringe benefits. [28] A
further distinction between statutory and occupational welfare is that,
through Parliament and other elected bodies, the social services are
accountable (in principle at any rate) to the public. Occupational
provision, on the other hand, is a part of the 'social policy' of private
enterprise which is only accountable to the share-holders. True, in so
far as governments have tended to see occupational benefits (primarily
pensions) as an important part of the policy for income security, occupational welfare has been increasingly subject to state regulation,
e.g. with respect to the preservation of pension rights. Moreover, in
countries with a strong social-democratic influence, notably Sweden,
the trade unions have been trying to narrow the gap between manual
and non-manual workers in respect of occupational benefits. [29] Despite
these developments, however, substantial differences of principle
between state and occupational welfare must remain which cannot be
legislated away.

Finally, it must be remembered that occupational welfare is not
peculiar to the private sector. The most ancient and venerable form of
occupational provision in fact belongs to the state as an employer. In
many European countries, including Britain, the civil servants were
the first group of civilian employees to receive pensions. [30] Since then
the rights of superannuation, sick leave, paid holidays and the like
have been extended to many other public employees, including
professionals such as teachers with their special schemes. From the
available evidence it appears that public enterprises do not differ substantially from private enterprises in their treatment of manual, non-
manual and professional and managerial staffs regarding occupational
benefits. [31] In so far as there is a broad similarity between the private
and public sectors, it supports the view that in capitalist society the
state is an integral part of the dominant values and institutions of
capitalism. In short, the influences stemming from the core institutions
and values are no less operative in the public sector.

Another form of welfare that has developed alongside the extension of public services and the taxation of incomes consists of fiscal benefits. Thus, the child tax allowances are an important form of child bounty in capitalist countries.[32] In Britain a child allowance for the low income tax payer was introduced in 1909. By 1920 it had been extended to all tax payers.[33] This tax concession for children antedated family allowances by nearly four decades. As is well known, these allowances cost the Exchequer far more than the family allowances. They benefit higher income groups far more and operate on principles much more generous than those underlying the family allowances.[34] To take another example: in 1968–9 tax relief granted to owner-occupiers on mortgage interest cost over £200m. Not a mean sum when we remember that council house subsidies cost only £235m. in that same year.[35] Until recently there was no ceiling on the amount of loan for house purchase on which tax relief could be claimed. Thus the purchase of a mansion was being subsidised by the taxpayer ostensibly as an inducement to home ownership.[36] These are but a few examples of the variety of tax allowances and benefits that seem to constitute an 'invisible' welfare state largely for the upper and middle classes. For as a rule the higher the income and higher the rate of tax paid, the more valuable is the tax concession. Thus in 1959–60 the top 1 per cent of the income earners received about 14 per cent of the sum paid out by the government as tax relief on life assurance premium.[37] Moreover, apart from tax reliefs and allowances granted to individuals there are indirect benefits accruing to higher income groups through tax subsidy on occupational pensions. The cost of these tax exemptions is apparently 'one of the best kept secrets of British public life'.[38] For 1968 the value of this subsidy was estimated at £800m. – nearly three times the Exchequer supplement of £300m. to national insurance fund in that same year.[39] According to one authoritative estimate, in 1971–2 the total tax relief on occupational pensions, mortgage interest, child allowances and life assurance amounted to about £2500m. – more than double the Exchequer contribution to public income maintenance services during the same period.[40] Cross-national data on fiscal benefits are hard to come by, but if Britain is any guide, what is involved here is not some marginal phenomenon but a form of income maintenance for the affluent on a lavish scale.

In sum, the social services, fiscal benefits and occupational welfare may be said to constitute the three main elements in the structure of welfare in advanced capitalist society. Each of these and their relationship with the others must be examined if we are to get a reasonable grasp of the dynamic relation between society and welfare under capitalism. Titmuss's pioneering work *The Social Division of Welfare*[41] was more concerned with establishing the lineaments of this three-fold division than with exploring its sociological significance. None the less Titmuss's work is full of pointers in this regard. At any rate, one of the themes implicit in his discussion is that these three elements of welfare show the complex intertwining between the economic (market) and the political institutions (democracy and the growth of state institutions) of modern capitalism, between social stratification on the one hand and the social recognition of needs and dependencies on the other. Titmuss rightly stresses the relevance of Durkheim's insight, namely that increasing social differentiation and specialisation result in a greater degree of interdependence. This insight, writes Titmuss, is of 'primary importance in understanding the development of systems of welfare'.[42] Unlike Durkheim, however, Titmuss also shows the way in which this increasing dependency and its social recognition still takes place within the stratified social order of capitalism.

The Development of Social Policy

Our discussion of the nature of welfare in modern capitalist society shows that the change from early to advanced capitalism cannot simply be seen as one of a widening scope of state welfare. Any attempt to explain the development of social policy therefore must come to terms with the three principal elements in modern welfare systems – the social services, fiscal benefits and occupational welfare. However, a good deal of primary research into the history of the two latter forms of welfare is needed before they could be incorporated into the account of the development of social policy. Meanwhile we have no alternative but to restrict ourselves to the social services. In short, we shall consider the degree of state participation in welfare as the most important variable, historically and cross-nationally, that needs to be explained.

As regards state welfare, the trend in capitalist countries over the last century or so is quite unmistakable. The 'nightwatchman state' has been superseded by some form of 'welfare state' everywhere. The extent of state participation varies but despite the ideological and cultural diversity of such countries as Sweden, Japan and the United States, the state has come to play a bigger part in providing education and social security everywhere. What accounts for this increasing state intervention? In the broadest sense the explanation has to be functionalist. The interaction between three developing elements, industrialism, capitalism and labour movement, has made a degree of state intervention almost inevitable.

First, then, advancing industrialism. (What follows here is a brief summary of arguments already met with in Chapter 3). With industrialisation, an increasing proportion of the labour force has been drawn out of self-employment, for example farming, into the labour market. As a result, more and more people have been exposed to the risks of unemployment, sickness, industrial injury and the like. Among other things, this has meant that once an income security programme has been started its quantitative growth has simply followed industrial development. Demographic and other changes typical of advancing industrialisation have generally meant an increasing proportion of senior citizens in the population.[43] The problem of retirement income has become more weighty. Increasing industrialisation has also meant progressively greater urban development, which in turn has highlighted the question of regulating the urban environment and intervening in the market for housing and land. Education is vital for the economic (necessary skills) and political (socialisation and social control) order of industrial societies. Thus the capitalist state has intervened early to ensure a modicum of education for the masses. It is in the case of education above all that the functionalist equation between the industrial society and state welfare is most evident. Thus nearly a hundred years before the New Deal that bastion of *laissez-faire*, the United States, had begun providing elementary schooling under public auspices.[44]

Second, capitalist development. To appreciate the significance of this point we have to remember that as an economic (financial, commercial and industrial) system, capitalism is world-wide. In the mid-nineteenth century, England was the only developed capitalist country. By the turn of the century Germany and the United States had emerged as powerful capitalist nations, soon to be followed by others. From its early days the capitalist economy has been plagued by booms and slumps. This is one of the major consequences of the contradictions inherent in a capitalist economy, one which Marx believed could be the system's undoing. However, so long as capitalism was relatively undeveloped internationally, economic fluctuations were mild and of short duration.[45] The world-wide development of capitalism changed this situation by multiplying the effect of the crises manyfold. The economic crisis of the inter-war years far exceeded in severity and duration anything that the down-swing of the trade cycle could produce during the infancy of capitalism. In conditions of advanced capitalism, therefore, the economic and political consequences of *laissez-faire* assumed disastrous proportions. To say this, however, is not to suggest that the scale and intensity of the disequilibrium made state intervention – for example the New Deal – 'inevitable'. What cannot be denied, however, is that the experience of the inter-war years and the Keynesian thinking that emerged out of this experience has played an important part in the development of state intervention in the economy generally and in respect of the income maintenance services in particular.[46] It should be noted, however, that the global nature of the capitalist economy is also likely to inhibit the development of too extensive or 'progressive' a system of state welfare in any individual country. This is particularly evident, at any rate in Britain, when social-democratic governments try to increase (or sometimes even maintain) public spending on the social services. No British reader needs to be reminded of the way the 'gnomes of Zurich' and other financial authorities ensure that we do not stray too far from a 'healthy' economic policy. In any case, too extensive a development of the public sector or of the social wage is likely to result in the flight of capital and other forms of crises of confidence. In short, it is important to bear in mind that the capitalist economic system is world-wide and that this has considerable implications for the social policy of an individual country.

Third, the labour movement. The emergence of manual workers as an organised sector of society can, in a sense, be seen as an integral part of the development of the political economy of capitalism. It is best, however, to treat the influence of the working class as an independent factor. The growth of trade unions and especially of labour parties is not simply a by-product of industrial development, like the smoke belching out of the factory chimneys. Indeed one of the ways in which capitalist development has differed is in respect of the degree of unionisation and the emergence of working-class parties. The labour movement is linked with the development of state welfare in many ways. First, in the growth of the labour movement the ruling classes have seen a potential threat to capitalism generally and to property in particular. This has encouraged reformist policies. The extension of the franchise and the development of labour unions and parties has often come together in such a way as to be highly conducive to policies of amelioration. Bismarck's social legislation and the social measures of Edwardian Britain are good examples. Second, the ruling classes have also seen social welfare legislation as an antidote to socialism, as something that would help to 'spike the socialist guns'. Third, labour movements have themselves put forward demands for social legislation as a means of improving the life-chances of the working people. And finally, democratic socialists have supported these measures as a step towards the ultimate goal of a socialist society. Indeed social democratic governments, for example in Sweden, Britain and New Zealand, have used the extension of the social services as a major strategy of social change.[47]

Perhaps it should be pointed out that in stressing the influence of the manual workers and working-class political parties we do not wish to deny the contribution of other social groups – for example, the professions and philanthropic and religious organisations – in the development of state welfare. While not wishing to belittle their role in any way, we must insist on the need to assign weight to the influence of various social groups. In our view, the decisive influence in the development of state welfare has been that of the trade unions and the labour movement as a whole.[48]

In sum, developments stemming from industrialisation, capitalist economy and the working-class movement taken together have largely been responsible for the decline of *laissez-faire* and the growth of statutory provision. But the timing and the scale of this development has been very uneven, and it remains true that capitalist countries vary a great deal in the extent of state responsibility and provision for social needs. How do we account for this variation? Again many factors are involved and in our view the most generally applicable as well as economical explanation is in terms of the inter-action between economic development and the class structure. Although all capitalist countries have certain basic economic institutions and processes in common they have begun industrialisation in differing international contexts and from very different socio-economic backgrounds. These factors have had a profound influence on the development of state welfare. Of particular importance has been the nature of the leading social class. Capitalist industrialisation has been initiated by at least two different social groups – the middle classes and the traditional aristocratic groups. The former – merchants, manufacturers, private entrepreneurs – are the 'classic' groups involved in pioneering industrial development, for example in Britain and the United States. The traditional groups have led the development, for example in Germany, Austria and Tsarist Russia and, in a different cultural setting, in Japan. The main difference between the two groups is that the middle classes are individualistic and anti-statist and have favoured a residual approach to social policy. The classic case of course is that of Britain in the nineteenth century and the United States before the New Deal, but similar attitudes and beliefs can be found elsewhere. By contrast, where the traditional groups have been ascendant, the ideological and political climate has been more favourable for a proto-institutional form of social policy. In such countries, the collectivist structures of control and the values of the leading social group have accorded with paternalism in respect of the workers' welfare. The state has therefore played a more positive part in meeting needs at quite an early stage of industrial development. This was the case, for example, in Germany and Austria in the late nineteenth century and Tsarist Russia in the early twentieth century.[49]

An important point that emerges from the distinction between these two types of industrialisation is that early capitalism as such cannot be equated with *laissez-faire*. The latter formed the economic and social policy of only one type of early capitalism, namely that development led by the middle classes. Elsewhere the state played an active part in promoting economic and social development. The German nation-state, for example, grew out of the consolidation of a host of principalities ruled by independent princes, Prussia being the foremost. Many of these kingdoms followed a mercantilist policy which included some state ownership of economic enterprises and fairly extensive state regulation of the economy. Bismarck's Germany, thus, inherited both material and ideological legacy of state collectivism and extended it further.[50] It is not surprising that Germany should have developed an institutional social policy quite early. This becomes even less remarkable when we remember that comprehensive schemes of social security have no necessary connection with the redistribution of income or similar changes in the relative position of the various social classes (see p. 110 below). It is the association of *laissez-faire* with early capitalism and its supersession with social-democratic governments in Anglo-Saxon countries that has given rise to the idea that state collectivism (whether nationalisation of industry or the provision of social services) constitutes some form of socialism. However that may be, the financing of Bismarck's social insurance scheme left little scope for the redistribution of incomes. It was largely financed by contributions from employers and employees with only a small state subvention.[51] And as an early observer of German social policy remarked, the employers' contribution was likely to be passed on to the consumers so that a substantial part of the total cost was borne by the workers themselves. He concluded: 'obligatory insurance, practised under state direction, is only thrift systematised and protected by ampler guarantees than can be offered by private action and commercial enterprise.'[52]

If the class dominant in the early phase of capitalist industrialisation shapes the nature of social policy initially, what influences policy subsequently? In our view the major influence is the strength of organised labour. Our thesis is that the higher the proportion of labour force unionised the greater the chances that the state will assume responsibility for basic needs. A high level of worker unionisation will, in short, favour the growth of state welfare. This can best be illustrated by contrasting Britain with the United States. Both countries industrialised under middle-class dominance, yet by the First World War Britain had taken important steps towards the welfare state while in America it was not until after the great depression of the 1930s that a government programme of social security was launched. Why was residual social policy undermined in Britain while it remained 'hegemonic' in the United States? The answer we would suggest lies in the far higher density of unionisation of labour as well as in the development of a socialist political movement in Britain.[53] In the absence of these factors middle-class social policies retained their hold much longer in the United States. Indeed throughout American industrial development the proportion of labour force organised in unions has remained a good deal lower than in Western Europe generally. The reasons for the much slower development of unionisation and the inability of socialist ideology to take roots are in turn related to peculiar American conditions, above all to immigration. Be that as it may, for our purposes it is sufficient to note the absence of

organised labour as an influential social group until at a very advanced stage of industrialisation. The persistence of a *laissez-faire*
social policy in the United States is often attributed to the uniqueness
of the American ideology of individualism.[54] On the other hand many
students of labour history and social welfare have noted that
American workers, indeed Americans generally, are not significantly
different in their attitudes from their European counterparts.[55] Indeed
it seems clear that, for example, if the United States has no national
health service, it is not because the American workers have preferred
to negotiate medical insurance plans with their employers or indeed to
rely on the market. It is rather because American labour has not been
sufficiently influential in overcoming traditional opposition, notably
from the American Medical Association, to state medical insurance.[56]
True, America seems unique in that the American Federation of
Labor (A.F.L.), the sole workers' organisation (i.e. labour federation)
from the late nineteenth century until the formation of the Congress of
Industrial Organization (C.I.O.) in the 1930s, not only held aloof from
schemes of state welfare but in fact opposed them.[57] This seems to
add weight to the idea of a uniquely American ideology of self-reliance
and distrust of government. But this explanation loses its per-
suasiveness a good deal when it is realised that A.F.L. remained a union of skilled craftsmen – principally white.[58] In other words the
A.F.L. can be seen as a rather extreme version of the exclusive craft
unions in Europe, notably Britain. Although the British craft unions
did not oppose social legislation, they were not the most enthusiastic
supporters of the social services.[59] Indeed, the friendly society
movement (workingmen's mutual aid insurance organisation), largely
a creation of the skilled craftsmen, favoured a harsh Poor Law policy
and was a bitter opponent of state schemes of social security, notably
sickness insurance and pensions.[60] This is not surprising when it is
remembered that economically as well as socially the skilled
craftsman tended to be far superior to the general labourer in the
earlier phase of industrial development.[61] And demands for a more
general working-class social policy – of which the social services were
a part – were not raised in Britain until after the influx of unskilled
workers in the ranks of organised labour.[62] Indeed the 'new model'
unions of mid-Victorian years provided friendly society benefits from
a subscription that was far too large for the unskilled worker.[63] In the
United States, it is true, the A.F.L. developed no comparable friendly

society activity nor did mutual aid in any other form make much headway.[64] But the A.F.L. believed in strengthening its market position through exclusiveness and collective bargaining with employers. It is not, I believe, an exaggeration to suggest that the ideology of the A.F.L. was only a somewhat more exclusive and American version of the skilled artisan's ideology elsewhere. Indeed a part of the thesis advanced here is that a high density of worker unionisation leads to more collectivist social policy partly because it transforms the less skilled workers, with a far more precarious market position in terms of wages and security of employment, into a pressure group. This did not happen in the United States until the 1930s.[65] However, this is not to suggest that the unionisation of the unskilled influenced the social legislation of the New Deal. Indeed if anything the causal relationship was the other way round. The New Deal legitimised unionism and collective bargaining as well brought a major social security programme into being.[66] It owed little directly to working-class pressure, and although organised labour has played a more important part in the subsequent development of state welfare, the results have not been very impressive.[67] Thus it should be quite clear that explanation in terms of the role of the working class is not a substitute for a detailed multi-causal explanation of the development (or its lack) of the welfare state in a particular country, in this case the United States.

Indeed the relationship between class, whether ruling groups or workers, and the welfare state cannot be seen in mechanical or 'deterministic' terms. Thus the pre-eminence of traditional ruling groups during a capitalist country's industrialisation does not ensure the rapid development of social services. Far from it. Rather the nature of the ruling class must be seen as an element that predisposes towards certain types of responses. For ultimately the welfare state is the result of elite response to certain problems of industrial capitalism – above all, and in the earlier stages, the problem of how to ensure the compliance of the broad masses to the capitalist social order. Thus it must be remembered that Bismarck's social policy was a part of his anti-socialist strategy; reform and repression went hand in hand.[68] In Tsarist Russia too social reform measures followed violent pressures from below.[69] Japan's case is also instructive. Here we have an example of a country which modernised under the aegis of a traditional class. Yet apart from education, social services remained

largely undeveloped until the Second World War.[70] True, in contrast
with the middle-class countries, the state played an active part in
promoting economic development in Japan. But state involvement and
activity did not extend to social welfare. Indeed the state pioneered
many industries only to hand them over to private enterprise later.[71]
Unlike Germany the Japanese rulers seem to have relied on repression
rather than reform in their dealings with the workers until the
mid-twentieth century.[72] However, to some extent, Japanese
paternalism in social policy took the form of company benevolence
towards the worker (see p. 96 above). As with the ruling class, the
presence of a large, organised working class does not *ipso facto*
guarantee a high level of state welfare, for, apart from other things, if
the working class is late in developing, as in the United States, the field
of welfare would be pre-empted by non-statutory organisations of
various kinds.[73] Pressure groups and vested interests defending the
status quo would be well entrenched and their opposition difficult to
overcome. Thus in Britain, the residual social policy of the nineteenth
century encouraged the growth of friendly societies which became one
of the strongest vested interests opposed to social insurance.[74] A more
recent example from Britain is that of insurance companies with a
large stake in private endowment assurance and occupational pensions – a phenomenon encouraged by the residualist social policy of
the Conservative government in the 1950s and early 1960s – which
means that any plans for state pensions must take occupational pensions into account. In short if the working class makes history it does
so 'under circumstances directly encountered, given, and transmitted
from the past'.[75] Moreover, in the United States, at any rate, socialism
as a political ideology has made little headway, and on the whole the
ideological hegemony of the bourgeois class has never been adequately challenged.

In conclusion we must emphasise that whilst the variation in the
class composition of capitalist countries is crucial for understanding
the development of state welfare, a comprehensive explanation of this
development must include many other things besides. The level of industrialisation measured by different indices (e.g. *per capita* income,
the proportion of labour force in non-agricultural occupations), the
degree of urbanisation, the degree of centralisation of government, the
demographic structure, political participation of the electorate and the
age of social insurance programmes are only some of the factors

which help unravel the complexities of social policy development.[76] However as we have stated earlier, this chapter focuses on society and welfare relationship in its broader structural aspects. We have stressed the role of social class as the most important general factor which accounts for the variation in social policy.

The Consequences of Social Policy

As in the previous section, our main concern here is with statutory welfare. The social services impinge on the social structure at numerous points and in a variety of ways. It is impossible to study the full range of these consequences. We must select and this selection (of what we consider as important, significant, etc.) will largely depend on our value preference. I have chosen to focus primarily on the consequences of welfare for social stratification, that is on class and inequality in its widest sense. The major questions I explore in this section are the following:

1. Do the social services reduce *class* differentials in income distribution?
2. Do the social services modify the class situation in any other way? In particular, do they affect class cleavage and conflict?
3. Do the social services enhance the power and privilege of those – the professionals and administrators – who man the services?
4. How far do the social services give rise to bureaucratism (i.e. bureaucratisation in an undesirable sense) and alienation?

Clearly, only some of these questions can be answered on the basis of empirical, quantitative evidence. The others either do not lend themselves to a quantitative treatment or else adequate data concerning them are not readily available. The discussion must therefore be largely speculative and exploratory. However, in my view these questions are both important and interesting and I hope an attempt to answer them, however tentative, will stimulate research and further discussion.

1. The belief that social services are egalitarian in their consequences rests largely on the assumption that they are paid for by the well-off (the few) and utilised by the less well-off (the many). In this

way they are supposed to redistribute income from higher to lower income groups. Undoubtedly the social services suggest a considerable potential for redistribution. As we have seen above, in most Western industrialised countries around one-fifth or more of the G.N.P. is allocated to the social services (see p. 95 above). Now there is no reason why this social distribution of income (largely a form of distribution in accordance with need) should not be egalitarian. Ideally this requires that the relatively well-off sections of the population pay for the services while the less well-off use the services. The reality is however very different. In a welfare state, with an institutional pattern of welfare, the social services tend to be universal. They are meant for all citizens and not just for the working classes. Rich and poor alike therefore use the services. However, there could still be a large element of redistribution if the services were financed by the higher income groups alone. In fact the rich as well as the poor pay for the services through national insurance contributions, income and inheritance taxes, rates and indirect taxes, e.g. excise on tobacco and alcohol. Thus the 'classless' nature of financing and use of the services within the framework of a predominantly market-based class society weakens the redistributive potential of the social services considerably. However, there would still be an element of redistribution, albeit small, if the richer sections of the community paid more in taxes than they received in benefits from the services. Whether and to what extent this happens has been the subject of a good deal of attention, at any rate in Britain.[77] However, the task of establishing the contours of the redistribution involved with any degree of reliability is beset with many problems.[78] The general conclusion to which most studies seem to point is that the extent of inter-class redistribution of income, i.e. from the higher to the lower socio-economic groups, is rather modest and that the nature of income transfer involved is far more of an intra-class or life-cycle variety.[79] In other words, the healthy pay for the sick, those at work pay for those without, the childless for those with children and so on, rather than the rich for the poor.

The limited nature of income equalisation between classes achieved by the welfare state is likely to disappoint those – the Fabians and others – who see the social services and taxation as major instruments of equality in capitalist democracies. What is more, time-series data leave little scope for optimism in this regard, for if cross-sectional data show that there is a modicum of vertical redistribution, time-series

data suggest that the extent of redistribution does not necessarily increase when a higher proportion of G.N.P. is allocated to the social
services. In Britain, for example, despite the Beveridge reorganisation
and the coming of the post-war welfare state, the combined effect of
taxation and the social services was not more redistributive in the
1950s than it was in the 1930s.[80] On closer examination this does not
come as a surprise. For what is involved in the change from a residual
or quasi-institutional to an institutional pattern of social services (as in
Britain during the 1940s), is, *inter alia*, the extension of the services to
the middle and upper classes. Unless the financing of the services and
the tax system generally are so adjusted that these groups pay more in
taxes than they receive in benefits there would be no redistribution as a
result of the extension of the services. Indeed this absence of
redistribution may be the precondition for the development of the
social services in capitalist society. The basic immunity of income distribution from the effects of the reallocation of resources may be the
price exacted by the upper and middle classes for accepting a substantial socialisation of distribution. However, this long-term stability in
the reward structure of capitalist society does not preclude short-term
fluctuations resulting from changes in government. It is no secret that
social-democratic governments generally favour redistributive policies
whereas governments of the right favour the opposite. As these
governments generally alternate in office, a see-sawing battle goes on
around redistribution. The point, however, is that this short-term fluc-
tuation takes place within the framework of a long-term stability.
Social services, then, do little to equalise the distribution of rewards
flowing from the institutions of market, private property and inheritance. Indeed this becomes clearer when the modest amount of
vertical redistribution achieved through the social services and taxation is put in its wider context. As Titmuss and others have shown, the
post-war years have seen the erosion of the tax-base of income and
wealth, in Britain and other capitalist countries, through the development of various tax avoidance techniques and fringe benefits.[81]
Studies of the impact of social services and taxation on incomes are
thus working with a concept of 'income' that leaves out many forms of
'command-over-resources'.[82] When these are taken into account the
redistributive impact of the social services appears slight or even non-
existent. As David Harvey explains, 'Policies that are designed to ac-
complish a redistribution of income may be offset by a change in

the ... definition and meaning of income and thus may return the distribution to the original position.'[83] In other words if the dominant institutions and values remain unchanged, reforms in one set of structures can be negated by 'compensatory' changes elsewhere.

If social services do not help to bring about greater equality of incomes do they at least reduce inequality in respect of specific life-chances, i.e. in respect of medical care, education, housing and income security? The answer here must be in the affirmative though even in this case the situation is far from simple and varies from one service to another. Historical comparisons are not easy to make but there can be little doubt that among other things, the free access and standardisation brought about by the national health service has vastly improved the chances of wage-earners and their families of receiving adequate medical care. On the other hand, class differentials in many other respects, e.g. infant mortality, show little change.[84] The case of education is somewhat different in that outside the state sector, there is a significant private sector with the prestigious 'public' schools catering unashamedly for the children of the upper and middle classes. Although there is a yawning gap between the educational resources of the state and the 'public' schools, perhaps the social distinction between the two is the more significant.[85] However that may be, historical data do not show a marked narrowing of class differentials in educational opportunity and attainment.[86] Housing presents a different picture again. If in medical care, and to a lesser extent in education, equality of life-chances can at least be seen as an objective of state intervention, this is clearly not the case in housing. Here the idea of a basic minimum of house-room and amenities rather than equality seems to have been the objective of housing policy. Gross inequalities, therefore, persist in housing (the council flat or the small terraced dwelling on the one hand and the stately home in the midst of extensive park and woodland on the other) but apparently cause little concern. None the less, to the extent that council housing and other government measures have resulted in providing a 'floor' in housing standards, extremes of inequality have been somewhat mitigated. Finally, the income maintenance services differ from the others in that whereas the latter are concerned with the distribution of a particular good or commodity, the former are concerned with the distribution of cash – money income itself. Naturally the main objective here has been security (through life-cycle transfers) rather than equality. Even so, the income maintenance services tend to provide a floor and in moderating the extremities of deprivation may be said to equalise life-chances in respect of security. Thus it is likely that the working-class aged suffered greater deprivation compared with their middle-class peers at the turn of the century than they do in the 1970s.[87] To sum up: our brief review of this question points to three things. First, the redistributive impact of the social services on the inequalities generated and sustained by the dominant institutions of capitalist society is slight. Second, increased allocation of national income to the social services does not necessarily result in greater redistribution of incomes. In short, the public as distinct from private (market) form of distribution is not necessarily egalitarian. Third, it follows that the superimposition of universal social services on the highly stratified social order of capitalism does not so much reduce inequality as alter its institutional nature.

2. To say that the social services have little effect on class inequality is not, however, to deny that they modify the nature of class in capitalist society in other important ways. The point is worth emphasising as it has generally been ignored by Marxists as well as sociologists. Very briefly, in so far as the development of the welfare state involves the intervention of the polity in the economy, the determination of the class situation of the workers by market forces alone (dramatised by Marx and analytically refined by Weber) no longer corresponds with reality. True, both Marx and Weber, and especially the latter, saw the class situation of the proletariat in ideal-typical terms. But the development of state intervention towards the provision of a minimum of income, health, education and housing (at any rate in principle; in fact, most welfare states fall short of achieving anything like this) pushes the reality further away from the ideal-type. Yet neither Marxists nor sociologists seem to have taken sufficient note of these changes in their analysis of class in advanced capitalist society. Marxists, mainly concerned with exploding the myth of achieving socialism via the welfare state, have stressed such factors as the meagre redistributive effects of the social services, their positive contribution to the smooth functioning of capitalism and the like.[88] In their eagerness to affirm that the essentials of capitalism have not changed, Marxists have tended to overlook the changes in class situation resulting from the development of state intervention in welfare.

Sociologists on the other hand, if they are not functionalists, have been more concerned with the relation between material conditions and status (*embourgeoisement*) and have generally been content to affirm the market-determined nature of inequality in capitalist society.[89] What has largely been missed out is the analysis of historical changes in the structure and processes of inequality, changes which render Marxian as well as Weberian analysis of the class situation of the workers to some extent dated as far as advanced capitalist society is concerned.[90] In short, there is a parallel between the assumption of perfect competition in traditional economic analysis and of purely market-determined life-chances in sociological analysis.[91] Each of these models is in some respects far removed from contemporary reality. Yet neither Marxist nor other class theory has come to terms adequately with the political determination of stratification under capitalism.

But perhaps the social services have influenced class in a more fundamental way by promoting social integration, i.e. helping to 'incorporate' the working class within the social order of capitalism. Early sociologists, notably Marx and Durkheim, were largely concerned with the transformation of a traditional, feudal type of social order into one dominated by quite a different set of values. For Marx, the problem arising out of this transition takes the form of alienation – not merely from work but in a wider sense, that is from society itself. It arises out of the individual's emancipation from the social and communal ties of a feudal society and his subjection to the harsh realities of the market place – the bourgeois world of impersonal, contractual and instrumental relationships. 'The bourgeoisie, wherever it has got the upper hand, has put an end to all feudal, patriarchal, idyllic relations. It has pitilessly torn assunder the motley ties that bound man to his "natural superiors" and has left remaining no other nexus between man and man than naked self-interest, than callous "cash payment".'[92] Elsewhere Marx writes of capitalism bringing into being 'a class in civil society which is not a class of civil society'.[93] The dehumanisation involved under capitalism, where the worker is treated as a mere factor of production and not as a human being, is a strong motif in Marx's indictment of capitalism. In Durkheim's work the problem appears as that of anomie – the deregulation of economic life, and the absence of a meaningful community that would effectively restrain the ego and integrate man with his society (see chapter 4 above). In Tönnies' classic formulation of *Gemeinschaft* and *Gesellschaft* the same motif of community appears in a different form (see p. 21 above). In short, with differing emphases the notion of a loss of community, the absence of integration, runs through a good deal of classical sociological thought. The fabric of the welfare state can be seen as a way of recreating community-like conditions in a bourgeois society (which is also urban and industrial) – a society that can only recreate it in the form of citizenship rights. This theme, identified with great sensitivity and skill by T. H. Marshall, has already been discussed above (see chapter 2). To recapitulate: social rights create a sense of 'belonging'; they have little to do with the abolition of class inequality. In other words, what is involved is primarily a return to status in a world that is and remains impersonal, contractual and highly unequal. In a sense, the position of the worker in the welfare state is analogous to that of the serf in the middle ages. The serf was part of a highly inegalitarian social order, but – and this is the main point – he belonged. He enjoyed a set of communal rights – the customary rights which gave him security of tenure, a *human* status, however lowly it may be. In a very different social setting, social rights reintegrate the worker, as citizen, with his society. These rights of welfare – the equivalent of property rights for those without property in capitalist society – symbolise the worker's belonging to the national community. In other words by recognising the worker as a human being with various rights or claims on the community, a measure of integration is achieved. Universal social services thus help in bridging the gulf between the 'two nations' of early capitalism. This humanising effect of the welfare state has been recognised by the Marxists and others on the left but more for its trivial nature – for what it *fails* to achieve rather than what it does achieve. It is seen as mere humanisation of the capitalist social order without any fundamental change. The sociological significance of this humanisation has not been grasped adequately. Conservative rulers such as Bismarck realised the significant part that social security could play in forging links between the modern capitalist social order and the working classes. For the social philosophy of conservatism as well as the intuition of the conservative politician suggests that the doctrine of class war and revolution is a minority ideology. It receives widespread support only in conditions where the masses are alienated from the existing society. And it is precisely this dealienative potential of the welfare state – realised at a small cost to the privileged classes – that is important in reducing conflict and tension and in promoting integration. In similar ways, if in widely varying social and political contexts, Bismarck, Lloyd George and Beveridge each set out to disprove the Marxist thesis that 'the working man has no country'. The common thread running through the major reforms associated with these names is the link between social legislation and the idea of nation and national integration. It is important, however, not to exaggerate the role of the welfare state in this respect. It is only *one* of the ways in which a sense of solidarity can be fostered in modern society. Clearly there are many social and psychological roots on which nationalism and national solidarity can thrive. All the same, a sharply stratified society where inequality is beginning to lose its legitimation may not be able to generate the requisite solidarity without amelioration. The question of legitimation, we must emphasise, is important. As both the United States and Japan in their different ways show, the welfare state is not a necessary condition for achieving national solidarity. On the other hand, there is no denying that it can make a major contribution in creating and reinforcing solidarity.

The welfare state may have contributed in reducing basic class cleavage and conflict in other, more direct, ways. The social services create a host of new interest groups that tend to cut across class lines. With the services available to everyone, social groups such as the old age pensioners, the widowed, the disabled and the like, irrespective of class, share common interests and problems in relation to social welfare. True, class differences stemming from the overall economic position remain important. None the less, the various interest groups created by the welfare state increase the complexity of stratification quite considerably. The relative simplicity of class and class conflict related to the individual's place in the productive process, gives way to a situation of greater complexity with a variety of interest groups competing for resources. This results in a certain fragmentation of class interests, in the development of sectional claims on resources which bypass class affiliation, e.g. students' claim for higher grants, old people's for higher pensions, owner-occupiers' for the retention of tax-reliefs. Indeed this can also result in a division of interests within a class; the interests of the council house tenants, for example, might diverge from those of their working-class peers who are owner-occupiers or live in privately rented accommodation. To quote Westergaard: 'The impact of the social services has tended ... to be divisive: to draw lines between different categories of workers ... social security provisions distinguish "the poor" from others; those who are given special help, on special conditions, from those who use only the standard services. That by itself is liable to foster mutual resentments.' [94] In short, state intervention is more likely to create sectional group interests of a kind which, to use Coser's phrase, prevent 'basic cleavages from emerging in society'.[95] Clearly, the overall importance of social class – for the life-chances of the old, the widowed, the disabled – is not in question. What is at issue rather is the new and varied form that it assumes through the interaction between the economic and political orders.

Weber argued that the extent to which class interest gives rise to concerted action depends partly on the 'transparency' of the class situation, that is how clear-cut and intelligible are the nature and sources of inequality. Marx made a similar point. In comparing 'cash nexus' and pure 'market' relations of early capitalism with relationships in feudal society Marx wrote, 'for exploitation veiled by religious and political illusions, it [bourgeois society] has substituted naked, shameless, direct, brutal exploitation'. Now it can be argued that capitalism overlaid by the welfare state once again draws the veil of 'political illusions' over the realities of class. The welfare state and the implied relationships serve to obscure the nature of the basic determinants of inequality. First, there is the sheer technical complexity of the nature of redistribution effected through the social services. Secondly, there is the fact that this modification of market distribution takes place on behalf of the underprivileged. The combined effect of these two may well be to weaken class consciousness.

3. In discussions of the relationship between the professions and social policy, the professions' influence on the development of the social services has been stressed a good deal.

How the social services have, in turn, affected the professions has, on the other hand, received far less attention.[96] In the absence of detailed empirical work, generalisation would be hazardous, and it is likely that the situation varies considerably between the services. But if the consequences of social policy for the medical profession in Britain are any guide, the professions have benefitted handsomely from the development of the social services. Perhaps the most recent example is that of social workers. One of the main consequences of the Seebohm

Report and the reorganisation that followed has been to enhance the power and privilege of social workers.[97] But this follows a well-established pattern: within the framework of a pressure group society, social policy is manipulated by the professions manning the services to their own advantage. This seems to be one of the features of the development of social services within a capitalist society where, thanks to the 'bias of the system', political pluralism helps the upper and middle classes – in this case the professions – in bending social institutions in their own favour. Medicine offers the outstanding example. As Titmuss has written in connection with the development of health services in Britain, 'of course the working classes have benefitted. But the middle classes have benefitted even more, and the medical profession most of all.'[98] In general the growth of socialised medicine, in Britain at any rate, has meant a vast improvement in the security of tenure and income of doctors and dentists.[99] It has also meant that control over the medical services has passed from primarily lay to professional hands.[100]

In general the development of the social services has led to greater centralisation and bureaucratisation; this has meant a decline in the power of lay interests, for example, the friendly societies and other voluntary organisations. But there is no reason why this process should result in the concentration of power in the hands of the professionals (or for that matter, the administrators). The main reason for this seems to be that the growth of professionalism and the wresting of control from lay hands has not been followed by any substantive (i.e. more than token) attempt to give countervailing power to the consumers.[101] Thus what seems to have happened is a net transfer of power to the professionals. The example of the medical profession in Britain shows how the nationalisation of services such as medical care within the social structure of capitalism can result in changes that are far from egalitarian. And if the notion of capitalism as a distinctive social system has any validity, then it is likely that the situation in other Western countries is not very different.

4. Our final point concerns bureaucratism or the 'dysfunctions' resulting from bureaucratisation. While the social services are integrative and help overcome the alienation of the working classes from the capitalist social order, the bureaucratism resulting from the development of these services seems to give rise to new forms of

alienation, i.e. in the relation between the citizen and the official.[102] Its main features are well known: the complexities concerning procedure and eligibility, the difficulty of obtaining information, indifferent or unhelpful attitudes on the part of the 'gatekeepers' and above all 'officialdom', namely the impersonal treatment of clients, lack of responsiveness to clients' needs and problems and rule-orientated rather than service-orientated behaviour. Undoubtedly conditions vary between the services and these negative features are more likely to be present in non-professional services, e.g. social security, housing and personal social services, than in medical care and education.[103] Whatever one may think of the privileges enjoyed by the professions generally, there can be little doubt that on the whole professional autonomy is anti-bureaucratic.[104] Where, therefore, the professional element is weak or absent, the services may have a greater tendency towards bureaucratism. The phenomenon of a large-scale, hierarchically ordered, complex organisation is of course not peculiar to public services or enterprises. Large private firms are no less bureaucratised in this sense than are public organisations. However, from the client's viewpoint the drawbacks of bureaucracy are likely to be especially pronounced in the case of public, including the social, services. The reasons for this are several. First, the social services tend to be monopolistic. Unlike privately provided services, therefore, the client cannot influence attitudes by threatening to take his custom elsewhere. (This is an ideal-type distinction. In practice, competition may be absent from private services just as an element of choice and competition may be present within the social services). Second, given the nature of the dominant values and institutions of capitalism, a cash payment relationship seems to put the exchange between the client and the dispenser of the services on a more equal footing than a 'free' service. This is clear if we compare, say, banking or insurance with social security in respect of the relation between client and dispenser. Third, the problem is more likely to be compounded with class differences. In non-monetary exchanges, the class membership of the client (education, occupation, speech, manners) may, paradoxically, be more important. The whole question of the nature of relationships involved in market and non-market forms of transaction is a complex and little-explored issue. Moreover, the professional nature of services such as medicine and education complicates the simple dichotomy between market and non-market services. None the less, even after

allowing for such factors it is quite clear that the alienative potential of
public services, stemming from various drawbacks of bureaucracy,
are considerable. Moreover, working people generally and the clients
in particular have little say in the running of the services. True, the
social services are ultimately accountable to the public through Parliament and local authority. But this is too remote and indirect a
relationship to be meaningful at the grass roots level. Nominally,
many British social services are run by 'volunteers'; effective power
resides in the hand of the professionals and higher officials.[105]
Moreover, the lay members of various management committees and
boards are often drawn from the upper and middle classes.[106] The
system of appointment to these bodies is far from open, and in any
case they seem quite remote from the everyday lives of the vast majority of the people.[107] Thus 'oligarchic' rather than 'democratic'
control seems to be the keynote of the administration of the social services. Steps taken to redress the situation have rarely gone beyond
'token' gestures. Moreover, given the nature of the 'totality' within
which the social services operate it seems doubtful if it could be
otherwise. The conclusion seems inescapable that the welfare state,
developed partly in order to overcome alienation and promote social
integration, gives rise to alienation in new forms.

Conclusion

This chapter has looked at the relation between capitalist society and
social welfare with respect to the nature of welfare, its principal determinants and some of its main consequences. The overall theme, implicit rather than explicit, has been the ways in which the class structure of capitalist societies has influenced the development, functioning
and the consequences of state welfare. The last section in particular
suggests that the logic of the capitalist social system is likely to
frustrate the pursuit of socialistic aims and values (greater equality of
rewards, democratic control and popular participation) through the
mechanism of the welfare state. This is not to suggest a relationship of
hard determinism (inevitability) but rather to point to the 'bias of the
system'. Moreover, as we shall see in the next chapter, some of the
problems and issues raised above are by no means confined to
Western capitalist societies.

Chapter 7

Welfare in Socialist Society: 'To Each According To His Needs'?

Our basic concerns in this chapter[1] are the same as in the last – the nature, development and consequences of welfare – but in the context of socialist society. Before moving on to substantive issues, however, a number of points need to be made clear. First, by socialist we mean societies, the U.S.S.R., for example, where the means of production are collectively owned. Our use of the term 'socialist' does not imply that these societies also display various other features of social structure, e.g. equality or democracy, associated with socialism. Undoubtedly, egalitarianism is one of the main elements of Marxian socialism – the ideological inspiration behind these societies. But how far this ideology informs the practice of welfare remains to be seen. This brings us to the second point, namely that the U.S.S.R. and most other socialist countries were economically backward at the time of revolution. This is a fact of considerable importance for understanding the social structure of these societies. For Marx's theories were largely concerned with the developed capitalist society. The distributive and other features of the post-capitalist (socialist) society envisaged by Marxism presuppose a high level of social and economic development. Yet revolutions inspired by Marx's teachings have occurred mainly in pre-industrial societies, notably Russia and China. As a result, the socialist revolution has become yoked to the industrial revolution. This fact of 'socialism in conditions of backwardness' is important for understanding the nature and development of welfare in these societies. Third, our discussion is focused on one socialist country, namely the U.S.S.R. True, some of the East European countries are industrially more advanced than the Soviet Union and provide a better example of welfare in advanced socialist society. But these countries, e.g. East Germany and Czechoslovakia, have gone through a long period of capitalist development. Their social services have a long history stretching back into the pre-socialist period, and three decades of socialism have not necessarily transformed the legacy of the past. Moreover, data on these countries are not as accessible as those on the U.S.S.R. Looking further afield, China and Cuba are certainly relevant as examples of non-soviet type of socialist development. But these countries are less developed industrially and their experience of socialist government is comparatively short. For these reasons we take the U.S.S.R. as the 'case study' of socialist welfare. Clearly we cannot generalise about socialist society from a single case. But in so far as we can speak of 'socialist' society as a type of social structure, the case of the U.S.S.R. is relevant for understanding the nature of welfare in socialist society. Finally, we must point out that as far as socialist countries are concerned, neither factual evidence nor discussions concerning welfare are plentiful. This means that many of our interpretations and generalisations have to be seen as tentative and exploratory rather than definitive.

The Socialist Conception of Welfare

Central to the socialist view of welfare is the notion that 'to each according to his needs' should be the guiding principle of distribution. In other words collective consumption – that is, typically universal, comprehensive and free social services such as health and education – constitutes the basic model of distribution under socialism.[2] Marxists believe that this form of equal distribution of the society's produce is possible only after private ownership of the means of production has been abolished, and the production and distribution of all resources brought under communal, e.g. state, control. Once this is done, the market, family and private property cease to be the basic institutions

institutional approach to welfare is, by and large, pragmatic. In this approach, the welfare state appears as a useful social institution – one that serves a number of purposes and which develops in a piecemeal and pragmatic fashion. In the normative conception, by contrast, the social services are not merely a convenience but an expression of the basic values of society. The 'clients' of the social services are not merely citizens entitled to a basic minimum of civilised existence under the auspices of the state but rather members of a socialist community whose needs are to be met to the fullest extent possible. Indeed the social ideology underlying this view of welfare regards the satisfaction of needs on the basis of equality as the main aim of production and distribution. From this angle the long-term objective of socialist societies is not simply to develop a generous system of social welfare but to become, so to speak, welfare societies *tout court*. Naturally these features are ideal-typical and as we shall see below the reality of Soviet welfare has been and still is very different from the model. But this does not mean that ideology is simply a window dressing. Indeed, there are good reasons for the gap between the ideal and the reality. First, even in the case of socialism developing from an advanced capitalist society Marxism envisages a transitional phase between the end of capitalism and the advanced phase of socialism or the communist society. During this transitional or early stage of socialism, distribution is still tied to work although the social services or need-based distribution forms a growing component.[3] Thus the notion of stages or transitional society forms an integral part of the ideology. Now the development of socialism from conditions of economic and social backwardness makes the gap between the ideal and reality a good deal wider and the transitional phase much longer. All ideologies contain an element of rationalisation and Soviet Marxism is no exception. But its influence on social policy in the past and its continuing relevance in the immediate future should not be underestimated. Indeed the ideological imperative – to move closer to the ideal of communism in the long run – is an integral part of the structure of socialist society, one of the features that distinguishes it from the industrialised West. Even in the most advanced welfare states under capitalism, social services as a whole remain an adjunct to the market system. Their scope is generally limited to the provision of a basic minimum (more true of housing and income security than of medical care and education), and in any case they are meant to complement rather than supersede the market system of distribution. Indeed state intervention is, in part, meant to shore up the institutions and structures of capitalism (see p. 102 above). In socialist society, on the other hand, the social services are part of a blueprint for creating a classless society. Their progressive development is the fulfilment of the promise of socialism. Abstracted out of their societal context, the social services in capitalist and socialist society may seem quite similar. But this outward similarity is misleading. Both in their meaning and in their origins, the social services in these two types of society differ profoundly. This fundamental difference arising out of the societal context must be kept in mind.

The Nature of Welfare in Soviet Society

Table 5 presents a profile of welfare in contemporary Soviet Union. At first glance, Soviet welfare seems remarkably similar to that of many Western countries, for example Britain (see p. 92). The nature of public provision in the two countries is strikingly similar, ideological differences notwithstanding. True, in some ways Britain is not typical of the advanced capitalist countries. For example, the national health service – universal, comprehensive, free and unrelated to sickness insurance – is closer to the socialist model of provision than medical care in most capitalist countries. Britain is also rather exceptional in its high proportion of municipal housing (see p. 94 above). But even after allowing for such factors, the broad pattern of the social services in the Soviet Union and the West is similar. However, this similarity is more apparent than real. The crucial difference, in a sense, lies in what the welfare profile does not show than in what it does. First, and this follows from what we said earlier, a 'snap shot' of the Soviet welfare system will not necessarily tell us the most important things about it; the position must be looked at in the context of development and change (we do this later). Secondly, a major structural difference between the way needs are met in the two social systems lies in the fact that the West is 'pluralistic' while the East is 'monistic'. In the former, the social services are one of a number of institutional patterns concerned with welfare; in the latter, the state is virtually monopolistic. Thus, when looking at capitalist welfare we identified three major structures through which needs are met: the social services, fiscal benefits and occupational provision. In the Soviet Union

TABLE 5: Soviet Welfare (*c.* 1970)

1. State services
   Income security

   Old age, invalidity and survivors' pensions; sickness,* maternity and work injury benefits (virtually universal scheme). Universal family allowances.

   Medical care

   Comprehensive and free health care for the whole population.

   Education

   Free and compulsory ten-year education;† pre-school, secondary, and higher education with maintenance grants.

   Housing

   Two-thirds of urban housing‡ publicly provided at nominal rent.

2. Proportion of national income spent on state welfare

   18.3 per cent§

3. Non-statutory welfare

   Some mutual aid among collective farmers; co-operative housing

* Collective farmers are excluded.
† Introduced in 1970 but unlikely to be fully operative for some years.
‡ *c.* 1960.
§ Expenditure on health, education and income security as a percentage of the net material product, a concept of national income somewhat different from the G.N.P. Data on health and income security (1966–7) are from *The Cost of Social Security 1964–66*, International Labour Office, Geneva, 1972, and on education from *Statistical Yearbook* 1970, Unesco, Paris, 1971.

and in socialist societies generally neither fiscal benefits nor occupational provision is of comparable scope and significance. The reasons for this are fairly clear. First, compared to the West the rate of income tax is quite low in socialist countries. In Britain, for example, direct taxes of all kinds took over 30 per cent of household income in the 1960s. In the U.S.S.R. the comparable figure was below 10 per cent.[4] The Soviet government prefers to raise its revenue largely by taxing state enterprises and collective farms and through indirect (turnover) taxes.[5] Moreover, since the government decrees all wages and salaries it has no need to resort to income tax in order to reduce income differentials. It can do this directly, by determining the wage tariffs. (This is true only up to a point. Taxation is necessary because the state determines the wage rates but not earnings.) However that may be, the fact is that first, the income tax is quite low. Secondly, the Soviet Union, unlike some of its East European neighbours, does little to reduce the tax liability of families with dependent children.[6] The Soviet Union does not appear to have anything comparable to the child tax allowance system in the West which, in Britain at any rate, operates on a system far more generous than the family allowances and helps the better-off families. In Eastern Europe, e.g. East Germany, where child tax allowances are given, the tax rates are still a good deal lower than in Britain,[7] and therefore the benefits appreciably smaller. True, a good deal of research is needed before any firm conclusions about fiscal policies in the East (including the incidence of turnover–taxes) and their implications for welfare can be reached. But available evidence suggests that in socialist societies the scope for income transfers through tax allowances is extremely limited. On the whole, it seems safe to conclude that the complex institutional maze concerned with tax evasion and avoidance and the various methods of income retention through fiscal policies have no counterpart in socialist society.

What is true of fiscal benefits is by and large also true of occupational welfare. The mini 'welfare states' of capitalist enterprises multiplying the rewards of occupational success through an array of fringe benefits has no counterpart in socialist society. True, since the beginning of the drive for industrialisation in the early 1930s, enterprises have offered some benefits to their workers. In the main, they seem to have taken the form of company housing – often in order to attract and retain key workers[8] – although holiday and health resorts and kindergartens should also be mentioned. But it does not appear that Soviet enterprises have the right to provide pensions, sick pay, maternity benefits, holidays and the like in addition to what is available through the social services. However, the mid-1960s have seen some major economic reforms in the Soviet Union and Eastern

Europe. Soviet enterprises are now expected to make a profit rather than merely fulfil physical quotas of production. To this end, the enterprises have been allowed greater freedom in managing their own affairs. They may, for example, determine wages (within prescribed limits) and provide housing and various physical or cultural amenities out of funds set aside from profits.[9] But freedom in matters of labour policy seems to stop short of the right to offer fringe benefits such as pensions and sick pay. How far these reforms pave the way towards the further development of enterprise welfare remains to be seen. What is quite clear, however, is that the socialist societies do not seem to have anything comparable to the occupational pensions of private and public enterprises under capitalism, with their bias towards generous provision for the managerial and professional employees. But this does not mean that the Soviet elites receive the same basic pensions as the ordinary citizen. Under Stalin's rule, special pensions were awarded to many high ranking military and civilian personnel as well as the cultural elites.[10] Later, a decree of 1956 laid down the law on 'personal pensions' setting a ceiling of 200 roubles monthly (the minimum pension for the Soviet citizen under the 1956 law was 30 roubles monthly and the normal maximum 120 roubles).[11] Special provision also exists for certain other categories of employees, notably military officers and academic and research personnel.[12] One effect of the special provision is to allow these personnel to draw a pension slightly higher than the normal maximum set for the Soviet citizen.

In Western societies, voluntary or charitable assistance and mutual aid are an integral part of the pattern of welfare. In the Soviet Union, the former hardly exists and the latter, with the exception of co-operative housing, is largely confined to collective farmers. As we shall see below, the Soviet regime excluded the farmers and the numerically small group of independent workers (e.g. craftsmen) from the state income security schemes. They were encouraged to provide pensions and other forms of assistance through mutual aid. Since 1965, however, collective farmers have been brought into the state scheme thus reducing the scope of mutual aid. On the other hand, the regime has encouraged housing co-operatives (formed by Soviet citizens to build or purchase apartments) recently as an additional source of supply of housing.[13] As regards voluntary and charitable work in the Soviet Union, its meagreness is not difficult to explain. This form of welfare, which played a prominent part in meeting needs in the West before the emergence of the welfare state and continues to thrive at present, presupposes two things: substantial income differentiation, and freedom of association and organisation. In the socialist society neither of these conditions obtain in a form comparable to the West. In particular, the monopoly of the party and the state is an important part of the political system of these societies. This rules out any welfare initiative outside the party and the various approved 'front' organisations. Voluntary activity seems to take the form of participation in the administration of services and in social work rather than the mobilisation of material assistance.[14] Needless to say, social policy pressure groups, e.g. the Child Poverty Action Group or clients' organisations, are largely absent from the Soviet scene. Information about voluntary organisations in the Soviet Union is hard to come by. There is little doubt, however, that such organisations are less numerous and a great deal less autonomous than in the West. Moreover, nothing comparable to the great charitable foundations of capitalist society does, or indeed can, exist in the U.S.S.R.

Turning next to the social services themselves, we must begin by drawing attention to certain features of socialist welfare that are not apparent from a look at the services themselves. Briefly these concern the virtual absence of private or market provision of various services. Thus unlike in capitalist countries, there are no high status, exclusive, private schools catering for the elite's children.[15] All children attend state schools which are generally run on comprehensive, i.e. non-selective, lines. Similarly all medical care is nationalised, although private practice is allowed. Thus a doctor may be consulted on a private basis but there are no private nursing homes, hospitals or beds.[16] However, it appears that the elites do receive preferential medical care and this takes the form of 'closed' clinics.[17] Thus as in the case of pensions noted above, a measure of stratification exists and operates through political rather than economic (market/income differential/private provision) structures. In housing, owner-occupation exists alongside municipal and other forms of public provision. But owner-occupation is more a legacy of the past than a form of new 'capitalism' (see below p. 138).The bulk of the owner-occupied housing is in the rural areas and comprises, mostly, the cottages of collective farmers. Again the mix between owner-occupation and public housing suggests a broad similarity with Britain and other Western countries. But a major difference between Soviet and Western housing is the far greater equality in housing standards in the U.S.S.R. True, a degree of privilege is enjoyed by the elites in the form of the use of country houses (*dachas*) and slightly bigger and better apartments. But this difference is paltry when set beside the fabulous and dazzling inequality of housing resources between the Kennedys, Rockefellers, Rothschilds and the like and a negro sharecropper in the deep South or a slum-dwelling Briton. The main point is that very clear and definite ceilings have been imposed by Soviet authorities on the amount of house-room that a Soviet citizen can enjoy.[18] No comparable restrictions exist anywhere in the West. This is not to deny that housing standards in the U.S.S.R. (even excluding the somewhat primitive rural sector) are a good deal lower than in the advanced Western countries.[19] But that is a rather different point from the *principles* underlying the distribution of existing stock of housing. Lastly we come to private provision for income maintenance. This is permitted and a sizeable minority of Soviet citizens have insurance policies – combined life and accident coverage is apparently a popular type.[20] Details of private insurance cover are hard to come by. But taken in conjunction with the tax system in the Soviet Union, it is clear that there is far less scope for private insurance to become a multiplier of income inequality.

Turning to the social services as such, we find that they present similarities as well as differences when compared with Western countries, e.g. Britain. Thus as in Britain, the health services in the U.S.S.R. are not entirely free and some charges are made, e.g. for drugs and appliances.[21] Indeed it is likely that the British system is more 'free' than the Soviet. Moreover, in at least one respect the British health service is far more 'normative' than the Soviet, namely blood transfusion. As Titmuss has shown, all blood in Britain is donated freely by volunteers; in the Soviet Union about half the blood is paid for.[22] Means tests too are a feature of Soviet social policy. Thus many educational charges – fees for nursery and boarding schools, costs of books and uniforms, school meals – are adjusted to family income. Alternatively, poor families are helped with the payment.[23] However, unlike Britain and many other Western countries, the U.S.S.R. has not instituted a system of public assistance for helping those not entitled to basic income maintenance benefits or with inadequate benefits. True, social security benefits have been improved very substantially since the mid-1950s, but it is most unlikely that all citizens are adequately provided for. The situation was of course much worse in the past when state pensions were meagre and the collective farmers were excluded from the state scheme altogether (see p. 134 below). However the Soviet authorities have never made any systematic provision for the relief of poverty although some help is given to the needy by the trade unions or local welfare offices.[24] Although no poverty surveys as such have been carried out in the U.S.S.R., studies of household living standards have begun recently and provide some clue to the extent of hardship. One Western writer estimates that using the Soviet authorities' own income standards for a modest level of living, about one-third of urban households in U.S.S.R. may be in poverty.[25] Indeed it is perhaps significant that a recent Soviet proposal for improved family allowances is a means-tested one.[26] This seems like an indirect admission that poverty exists and that one way of overcoming it may be to 'concentrate resources where they are most needed'. Little is known about the attitude to means test and about the problem of stigma more generally in the Soviet Union. In the absence of a general system of public assistance, the means tests have so far operated in the interstices of the main services. However, there is some evidence to suggest that Soviet society is not immune from the stigma of poverty and means test.[27] Naturally we must be cautious about looking at means tests in a mechanical fashion. Its 'meaning' can differ widely depending on the social, historical and administrative context and it could be that in the Soviet Union and Eastern Europe it has not the same stigmatising effect as in capitalist countries generally. However that may be, it cannot be denied that as regards income inequality and poverty, capitalist and socialist societies share some features in common. The main difference seems to be that private ownership of the means of production and the great concentrations of wealth resulting from it are absent from the socialist society.[28] But in respect of the division of labour and related income differentials, capitalist and socialist societies are broadly similar.[29] In so far as poverty is defined in relative terms it is, at bottom, a problem of material inequality and the Soviet Union and other socialist societies are by no means immune from it. Moreover, the various cultural and social advantages which often enable the middle classes in capitalist society to profit disproportionately from universal social services, notably education, are also present in socialist societies though not necessarily to the same extent.[30] Indeed these are but a few examples of a range of structural and cultural features – related to the level of industrial and economic development and perhaps to some more enduring features of human societies, for example the family – common to both societies. However, the differing economic, political and ideological systems in which they are enmeshed gives them a characteristically different quality.

In the discussion above, we have not been concerned with Soviet social policy in any detail. Rather we have pointed out some of the relevant similarities as well as differences between British and Soviet social services. One thing is clear. Soviet welfare falls far short of the ideal state of affairs envisaged in Marxian socialist ideology. Yet as we have mentioned earlier, this ideology is not unimportant and continues to have a major influence on Soviet social policy. There are, however, other influences – other considerations which pull away from the idea of need-based distribution. To appreciate this interplay between ideological and other factors we must look at the development of Soviet social services briefly.

The Development of Welfare in the U.S.S.R.

In capitalist countries, the social services have developed in a piecemeal and pragmatic fashion – largely as the result of *ad hoc* responses to various shortcomings of a *laissez-faire*, market society. In socialist societies, on the other hand, their development has been far more deliberate and planned and, above all, inspired by Marxian ideology. In the West change has occurred in the context of political and ideological pluralism. By contrast, socialist societies remain 'monistic' in both these respects. Policy has been, and on the whole continues to be, determined by the top leadership in the context of a unitary social ideology.

At the very outset of the revolution the Bolshevik leaders proclaimed a policy of extensive social provision for basic needs. As regards income security, within a few days after the revolution, the new government promised comprehensive non-contributory social insurance to cover all wage and salary earners as well as the rural and urban poor.[31] As regards medical care, a Health Commissariat was set up in 1918 and one of its major functions, spelled out at the Party Congress next year, was to ensure 'free and qualified medical and pharmaceutical assistance' to all.[32] The same Party Congress also decreed universal and compulsory education to the age of seventeen.[33] The policy objectives in housing were less explicit but the general aim was to secure an equitable distribution of existing accommodation and to provide housing as a social service.[34] This programme of welfare is of course very close to the normative model. Its realisation, however, was another matter and early Soviet practice fell far short of ideology. Within a decade of the revolution it became clear that given the con- ditions in Soviet Russia – economic and cultural backwardness, vast peasant population, the ravages of war followed by those of the civil war, and the need to 'go it alone' as a socialist country – the kind of social provision envisaged by the leadership could not be realised for a long time to come. Added to this were various considerations related to production and work incentives which became paramount with Stalin's drive for industrialisation. The upshot was a fairly large divergence between the ideological model and the reality.

Soviet social policy development may be conveniently divided into three phases: the post-revolutionary phase, roughly lasting a decade from 1917; the Stalinist-industrialisation phase spanning roughly the three decades from 1926; and lastly, the post-Stalinist phase, from about mid-1950s to the present day. Though an over-simplified periodisation, it is none the less helpful in discerning some of the major trends in policy, especially with regard to social security. The first period may be described as essentially 'utopian' and ideological and beyond this characterised by *ad hoc* and improvised policies to suit changing situations, e.g. war communism, New Economic Policy. It was also characterised by a great deal of experimentation, for exam- ple, in education. On the whole, while the basic objectives and ideals of social policy were clear, the actual situation was one of flux. By the mid-1920s, however, Stalin's view of 'socialism in one country' was gaining ground and 1928 saw the beginning of Soviet industrialisation under the first five-year plan. During the phase that began, ideological fervour was eschewed in favour of a pragmatic, if bureaucratic and authoritarian, approach to social policy with the eyes of the leader fixed firmly on production and various measures thought necessary to stimulate industrial progress. During this period Soviet social services began to take definite shape and if it was a time of large-scale depar- tures from the principles of socialist welfare it was also a time when the social services were consolidated. The third phase, like the previous ones, has been shaped by political as well as economic factors. It begins with the death of Stalin and with various measures aim-ed at the de-Stalinisation of Soviet society but coincides with the emergence of an urban-industrial society in the U.S.S.R. There are, of course, many continuities in policy as well through these phases. Thus in the post-Stalin period, questions of production, work incentives, labour discipline and the like have not, by any means, been ignored. But on the whole the social services, in particular the income maintenance services, have become more closely geared to need. There is a return to some of the ideological goals of the early Bolshevik period.[35] The leadership has been attempting to strike a balance between work-oriented and need-oriented social provision. While there seems to be a good deal of emphasis on the latter it must be remembered that there is no hard and fast line separating the two. The motivation is often mixed. Improved social provision is often ex-pected to have an economic pay-off.

Against the backdrop of the three phases of social policy outlined above, let us look at the development of specific services – income maintenance, medical care, housing and education – briefly.

(a) Income Maintenance The income security system envisaged by Bolshevik leaders was to be universal (cover all members of the com-munity), comprehensive (meet all major forms of income needs), ade-quate (high level of benefits), and as of right (without any special con-ditions of eligibility, e.g. work record or contributions).[36] To some extent these principles informed policy in the early years. But the stable system of income security that emerged in the late 1920s in-volved some notable departures. Thus universality was abandoned when social insurance (which was non-contributory) covered only the 'employed' section of the labour force, leaving the vast majority of the working population – the 'independent' workers such as the peasants, artisans, home workers and the like – to fend for themselves through mutual aid.[37] The abolition of unemployment benefits in 1930 was a retreat from the principle of comprehensive protection against income risks. Earlier, benefits such as sick pay and invalidity pensions had been paid without imposing any conditions such as years of service.[38] But in 1926 sickness benefit became conditional on the evidence of work record. Old age pensions, which began in 1928 (at first for cer-tain classes of wage earners only but later extended to other workers and employees and by 1937 to the whole of the 'employed' pop-ulation) required twenty-five years of work record for eligibility.[39]

Thus the principle of income security as a social right was set aside in favour of a work-related system of security. Adequacy of benefits, at least in relation to wages, fared better. But income maintenance services were linked more firmly to work incentives and production. The unproductive population − the old and the disabled − received low priority and benefits for this part of the population, which alone catered for need in the true socialist sense, were allowed to be whittled away by inflation. By the end of the 1930s they had become grossly inadequate.[40]

Table 6 gives a welfare profile of the U.S.S.R. *c.* 1950. From this we can see that despite major departures from the ideological model an impressive network of services had been built up. That the income maintenance services were far more developed in the U.S.S.R. than in Britain or the United States at a comparable stage of industrial development is quite clear if we look at the position in Britain in mid-nineteenth century (p. 92 above). The situation in the United States at the close of the nineteenth century was similar.

Major reforms in Soviet income security came in 1956 and in 1965. The earlier date saw the beginning of a major overhaul of the Soviet pensions system resulting in a vastly improved and a great deal more egalitarian system than before.[41] It should be noted however that eligibility and the size of pensions are still linked to years of service; most other benefits are also related to work record.[42] In 1965 the collective farmers, left out of the state social security system since its inception, were at last brought into the scheme. They became eligible for old age and disability pensions.[43] In general during the post-Stalin period benefit levels have been raised appreciably and conditions of eligibility liberalised. This trend continued throughout the 1960s.[44]

(b) Medical Care In Tsarist Russia public provision for medical care had become established on a limited scale.[45] Hence the nationalisation of medical resources and the employment of doctors on a salaried basis after the revolution was not such a fundamental break from the past. By 1920 socialised medicine had become accepted and the initial opposition from sections of medical profession overcome. The Health Commissariat, set up in 1918, had the status of a ministry and was charged by the party with the unification of medical and public health work and with the development of adequate health care.[46] During the early years the emphasis was very much on environmental, preventive and anti-epidemic measures. But from the early 1920s the problem of

Soviet population. This consisted of members of the former ruling classes (for example, landlords, bourgeoisie, nobles, Tsarist officials, merchants, Kulaks, Tsarist army offices) who were excluded from social insurance and hence technically from the health services. Health services were not withheld from this section of the population. But there is little doubt that these groups were discriminated against and had to rely on private treatment.[48] The 1936 Constitution at last gave a formal guarantee of free medical care to all Soviet citizens. Next year the insurance connection was severed and health care, like education, became a publicly provided service for all. The retention of private practice was one concession made to the medical profession which also enabled many members of the former ruling classes to receive medical care. However, the high rates of tax on private earnings provided little encouragement for its development. In the 1930s apart from a few older and eminent physicians all doctors were said to be state employees though some combined private practice with their public duties.[49] The post-war years have seen no major changes in Soviet health policy. In towns, the polyclinics or health centres and the hospitals constitute the backbone of health provision albeit industrial health services are also well-developed. The feldsher-midwife post and the smaller rural hospital, often attached to one or a group of collective farms, provide the primary stage of health care while more advanced and specialist treatment is available in the larger district hospitals and polyclinics.

This brief sketch of Soviet health services cannot even pretend to describe the vast and complex network of administrative, medical and para-medical organisations which any comprehensive health service in the world would entail today. But our aim was to offer a thumbnail sketch of a service to illustrate the general policy development. True, unlike income maintenance medical care does not show any shifts in policy through the three periods in Soviet social policy identified earlier. Naturally generalisations about policy rarely hold good in the same way for all social services. It should be noted, however, that the exclusion of collective farmers from income security services has its counterpart in medicine. Social insurance, which was the institution through which the urban worker and his family received medical care until 1937, did not include the peasantry. And while the rural population did receive medical care the vast gulf between rural and urban facilities was a *de facto* admission of 'double standards'. Thus in 1933, apparently 'one doctor in the countryside was handling about 14,200 people compared to only about 750 in the towns'.[50] Moreover, during the late 1920s and the 1930s, economic aspects of health protection received greater priority, and health planning was geared to raising labour productivity. There is also evidence that the physician's work was tightened up during this period and that medical decisions were over-ruled in the interests of production thus affecting the health and safety of the working population.[51] Policy concerns during the post-Stalin period suggest a 'normalisation' in this respect. The economic contribution of health services continues to be stressed but as a part of the wider objectives of medical care.

(c) Housing Following the revolution, a party decree abolished all private ownership in land but did not affect home ownership. The smaller owner-occupier's right of ownership – in towns as well as in the countryside – was respected.[52] Indeed, even of the larger housing stock only a small proportion was at first nationalised, leaving the bulk of the housing in the hands of various social groups – the nobility, the clergy and the bourgeoisie – about to be 'liquidated'.[53] Many of these houses remained in the hands of their owners though often accommodating the workers. Rent policy zigzagged through the early years but as one specialist on Soviet housing puts it 'since rent was regarded as a capitalist device for the exploitation of workers, its abolition became the ultimate goal of Soviet housing policy'.[54] Rents for municipalised as well as private housing were kept very low and varied according to income. Through lack of repairs, the absence of any incentives to landlords to improve their dwellings and through general lack of management existing housing stock continued to deteriorate. By the mid-1920s about half of the urban housing had been taken into the public sector.[55] Both local Soviets and state industries built new housing but during the drive for industrialisation resources were directed to investment and among the social services housing received low priority. While industrial development brought increasing numbers of people to towns, building hardly kept pace resulting in overcrowding and deterioration of housing standards generally.[56] Despite increasing municipalisation and building by the state for letting, nearly a third of the dwellings in urban areas remained owner-occupied in 1950.[57] Meanwhile in the countryside the farmers continued to own their small cottages usually built by themselves. The extensive destruction and damage resulting from the

Second World War had to be made good in the immediate post-war years and it is only from about the late 1950s that housing and house-building has received high priority. The major building programme is that of public housing but home ownership through co-operatives is also being encouraged. However, it accounted for less than 10 per cent of the total building programme in the late 1960s.[58] Some of the East European countries are tending to move towards an economic rent policy (supplemented with rebates for those in need) but the Soviet policy of charging nominal rent for state housing shows little change.[59] Thus it is only now that housing is emerging as a social service, i.e. an increasing proportion of Soviet citizens are being provided with satisfactory dwellings at a nominal rent.

(d) Education Early Soviet effort in education took the form of various crash programmes, such as the campaign for adult literacy, meant to raise the educational level of the working people. In principle education to the age of fifteen became compulsory but in practice even in urban areas compulsory education was only partially implemented.[60] One of the primary aims of early Soviet policy was to eliminate the Tsarist system of education, primarily geared to the needs of the elite, and to extend education (in various forms) to as wide a stratum of the working population as possible. In this the Soviet policy was largely successful. But compulsory education made limited headway. In the twenties the majority of the children at school received only a four-year education.[61] Moreover at this time Soviet education was characterised by a great deal of experimentation. Various theories of 'deschooling' and democratic control of education by the pupils themselves were being debated with vigour.[62] The beginning of the industrialisation drive and five-year plans spelt the end of this highly interesting and original, if somewhat chaotic phase in respect of children's schooling. Through a series of party and government decrees, education was organised along more conventional lines with the manpower needs of the industrialisation programme exerting an important influence on educational reorganisation.[63] As a result, the four-year primary school became effectively compulsory. The Soviet Constitution of 1936 affirmed the right of citizens to free seven-year education.[64] But it was only after 1949, when seven-year education was declared compulsory, that this became a reality for the Soviet children although in rural areas a sizeable proportion of children continued to receive a shorter education well into the 1950s.[65]

Through a series of measures the revolution opened up secondary and higher education to children of workers and peasants. Prominent among these were the abolition of fees, waiving of academic entrance requirements, provision of a variety of pre-university preparatory education and, not least, stipends and grants.[66] However in the thirties there was a general tightening up of the system and beyond the elementary stage the familiar pattern of selective secondary and higher education based on examinations became firmly established. A major departure from a socialist policy of education occurred in 1940 when tuition fees were introduced in selective secondary schools and higher education institutions (hitherto all education, with the exception of nurseries, had been free). However the fees were low and a wide variety of needy groups were exempted from payment.[67] Some Sovietologists have seen the imposition of fees as a part of the general trend against equality during Stalin's rule. Specialists on Soviet education however tend to reject this view. De Witt's explanation – that fees were intended to ensure serious motivation [68] (especially on the part of the students from well-off homes) – seems rather more plausible.

The post-Stalin years have seen some interesting moves in educational reform. Fees were abolished in 1956 as part of the policy of egalitarianism in the wake of Stalin's death. This was followed in 1958 by Khruschev's educational reforms. Among other things, they were intended to combat the 'academicism' and 'elitism' of selective secondary education by combining work and study. The reforms also attempted to encourage admission of students with work experience into higher education. However these measures, aimed at 'Polytechnicisation', were not very successful and Kruschev's fall from power in 1964 saw a gradual reversion to the earlier pattern.[69] Meanwhile compulsory education was extended to eight years in 1958 and at the end of the 1960s the Soviet Union was poised for a ten-year programme of compulsory schooling.[70] Let us conclude this all-too brief outline of educational policy by drawing attention to some of the differences between the U.S.S.R. and the West. First, in the U.S.S.R. a higher proportion of children from peasant and worker backgrounds reach selective (i.e. academic) secondary and especially higher education.[71] Second, a far higher percentage of people at work seem to benefit from part-time education and various training programmes run by industry.[72] Third, admission quotas and other forms of positive discrimination employed in Soviet higher education from time to time in favour of disadvantaged groups (e.g. peasants and workers, national minorities) has helped to equalise educational opportunity quite considerably.[73] On the other hand, it should be noted that in the U.S.S.R. the children of the intelligentsia or the middle classes, like their peers in capitalist society, enjoy many advantages over children of the manual workers. This is reflected in the continuing disproportion between the educational chances of children from different social strata.[74]

The brief survey of Soviet welfare development we have presented shows a number of things. First, the influence of Marxist ideology as shown in the Bolshevik objective of developing a network of universal, comprehensive and adequate services. Second, the constraints on this ideological goal stemming from the low level of economic development. These took the form of lack of resources and the difficulties of developing a network of social services in a predominantly rural and peasant society. Third, the distortions of priority resulting from the crash programme of industrialisation under the Stalinist regime. Fourth, the continuing strength of the idea of egalitarian social services as shown by the reforms of the post-Stalin era. Finally, also the continuing influence of economic and productive considerations. Indeed in a new form this may well be a major brake on the further development of social services. For although the post-Stalin era has seen a major expansion of income maintenance services and a general affirmation of welfare objectives, at present the Soviet Union does not seem to be spending much more on the four main social services than many Western countries.[75] Thus as far as the future of the social services is concerned the question is whether communal consumption in various forms would continue to grow. In the early sixties, party policy under Khruschev envisaged a continuing expansion of communal consumption in various forms, its share rising to about half (from about a quarter) of total consumption expenditure by 1980.[76] This policy formed a part of Khruschev's grandiose programme of transition to communism over two decades. Some of the major assumptions of this policy, e.g. that the U.S.S.R. would overtake advanced capitalist countries, notably the United States, in many branches of production, have proved totally unrealistic. Since Khruschev's fall from power much less is heard of transition to communism in the foreseeable future, and his successors have been following a far more cautious policy. While expansion of the social services remains a part of Soviet policy, the leaders' main concern seems to be with raising output and productivity generally and providing more goods and services for private consumption. Soviet economic reforms of the sixties, which give greater autonomy to the enterprises and expect the enterprises to be profitable, have been mentioned earlier. These and other recent measures aimed at improving economic efficiency and productivity rely, mainly, on material incentives. This, in effect, means continuing (and perhaps wider) income differentials as well as an increase in the supply of consumer goods and services (especially household durables and cars) which may be purchased out of higher earnings.[77] The logic of Soviet economic strategy seems to favour the expansion of private rather than communal consumption. However recent trends are somewhat conflicting and it remains to be seen if there is a pronounced shift towards private consumption. It is tempting to read a form of 'convergence' between capitalist and socialist welfare (both systems being pushed towards a mix of private and public consumption) in the light of these developments. However, it seems unlikely that Soviet leaders will abandon ideological goals easily. First, the 'building of socialism' or the 'transition to communism' is a major objective of Marxist leadership in all socialist countries, an objective which gives the party-state its legitimacy. Second, the exercise of power by the party bureaucracy depends on its control over the disposal of the national product. Communal consumption enables this control to be maintained directly over a large part of the resources in a way that private consumption does not. Thus to a large extent the legitimation and exercise of power by the political elites in socialist society is bound up with the existence of a substantial public sector under the direct control of the party and with delivering the goods in an ideological as well as material sense. The leaders cannot abandon ideological goals easily and Marxist ideology is likely to remain an important influence on the development of welfare in socialist society. It must also be remembered that decision-making in the U.S.S.R. and other socialist countries is not based on representative bodies and open lobbying and group conflicts typical of Western society. In short, the socialist leaders are much less constrained (at least directly) by various group pressures and have a good deal of leeway to act in terms of, or in the name of, ideology. In sum, then, the 'dynamics' of socialist welfare development differs in important respects from that of the West.

The Consequences of Welfare

How do the social services affect the social structure? When discussing this question in the context of capitalist society we concentrated on class and inequality in the wider sense. While the relation between the social services and inequality is also relevant in the context of socialist society, the implications are somewhat different. Unlike the capitalist system, incomes under a socialist system, for example in the U.S.S.R., are not generated through the market. The government controls wages and salaries directly. This wage determination is the main instrument for income equalisation. Social services are, therefore, potentially far less significant as a device for redistribution than under capitalism. None the less, like capitalist countries the U.S.S.R. also has a form of primary income distribution related to the division of labour and production. In the past this income differential has been quite substantial and broadly comparable to that of Western societies. Social reforms in the fifties and the sixties have reduced the differentials in wage-rates appreciably and on the whole they now seem less wide than in the West.[78] However, if wage-rates are controlled, earnings are not (there is no ceiling on earnings), or at least not directly. Moreover the economic reforms of 1965 have introduced the payment of a bonus linked to the profitability of the enterprise which can make a substantial addition to basic wages.[79] In short, while the small 'hard core' of the wealthy – millionaires and the like – typical of the West do not exist in the U.S.S.R., the incomes accruing from work are only slightly less unequal than in the West. It is of interest therefore to know how the 'social' distribution of incomes affects the occupational or 'economic' distribution. Does it reduce income differentials connected with occupation? In other words, the calculus of who pays and who benefits from the social services, familiar in the case of Western countries, would also be relevant for socialist countries. So far, however, such studies of the impact of taxes and social service benefits on income distribution are not available. What existing studies show is that the social services are redistributive – that is, they benefit the low-income groups more.[80] What these studies leave out of account, however, is the incidence of the various taxes through which the services are financed. A review of the literature on Soviet taxation suggests that the absence of a market economy, if anything, makes it more difficult to compute the incidence of taxation. There is little doubt, however, that as with the social services under capitalism, a good deal of the redistribution involved is 'horizontal' – that is, a form of life-cycle transfer. Certain features of socialist welfare, however, suggest a larger potential for vertical redistribution. Among the social services, transfer payments, such as pensions and sickness benefits, are less redistributive than services in kind, such as health or education. This is because, in capitalist as well as socialist countries, the former are wage-related benefits whereas the latter are not. Hence a country spending relatively more on social services in kind is likely to have the more redistributive social policy. In this respect the socialist countries seem well ahead of the West. State provision of housing at a nominal rent as well as other forms of subsidised consumption, e.g. gas and electricity (not normally considered as a part of the social services), tends to add considerably more to the real income of the Soviet worker.[81] On the other hand, as we have noted earlier, some services, e.g. higher education, are far more likely to benefit the higher income groups. Moreover it has been argued that in other areas of communal consumption too, for example housing, the higher income groups tend to benefit more. This is mainly because in a politico-administrative (bureaucratic) system of allocation of scarce resources, those with power and influence (generally also the higher paid) are able to bend the rules and manipulate the system to their advantage.[82] To some extent then communal consumption can act as a concealed multiplier of inequality. Indeed this is one reason why some socialist economists advocate a wider dispersion of wages together with a far greater use of the market mechanism in the distribution of services. In this way, they argue, at least the extent of inequality will be brought fully into the open and concealed income subsidies to the better off would be stopped.[83]

One of the consequences of state welfare that seems common to both socialist and capitalist societies is its effect on the attitudes of the working people generally. Put simply, it is that the social services help to 'incorporate' the masses into the existing social and political order. Thanks to the social services, the state, whether capitalist or socialist, gains considerably in legitimacy and support. We have explored this theme at some length in the chapter on capitalist society. As regards socialist society, perhaps the most direct evidence on the legitimating role of state welfare comes from the Harvard survey of Soviet refugees.[84] Reporting on the result of the survey Inkeles and Bauer write, 'It is evident from both the quantitative data and the qualitative impressions gathered from the personal interviews that the refugees most favour those aspects of the Soviet system which cater to their desire for welfare benefits. Such institutions form the corner-stone of the type of society they would like to live in.'[85] After the refugees had sampled life in the West (The United States and West Germany) for a while, they (especially the U.S. sample) expressed even stronger support for 'all three social welfare features of Soviet society – the system of education, the health programme and workers' benefits'.[86] Indeed the Harvard research team seems to have been deeply impressed by the widespread and strong support for these features among all types of Soviet refugees.

> Even the peasants, the group most hostile in their attitude towards the Soviet order and the group which in fact was most deprived under the Soviets, show a surprising tendency to acknowledge the achievements of the regime in these areas. . . Those who experienced arrest and those who had no contact with it, those who were forcibly evacuated and those who fled the Soviet authority of their own volition were alike in high support for the principles of the welfare state.[87]

In a different context radical thinkers such as Marcuse have emphasised the role of mass consumer goods and the welfare state in blunting the edge of opposition to the social order in advanced industrial society.[88] The argument could be developed a step further by suggesting that if in the West the dominant role in this respect is played by private consumption, in the Soviet Union the social services play a comparable part. Thus it appears that in socialist countries the party leaders and the workers are often united in their support for 'social' and egalitarian forms of distribution against the reformist intelligentsia who would like to see 'economic' and 'market' principles of distribution given more weight.[89] The security and egalitarianism of the social services probably help to bind the working people to the ruling groups. In this way the leadership is able to thwart demands for fundamental economic and political changes. Moreover, the idea of a continuing growth of communal consumption is also a source of political legitimation. In short, the pursuit of the classless society – distribution in accordance with needs as the ultimate aim of social development – also contributes to the support for the regime.

The relation between the professions and the social services is an important aspect of society-welfare relationship. Here the situation in socialist societies differs fundamentally from that under capitalism. In capitalist society, we noted earlier, the professions appear to have enhanced their privilege and power in the course of the development of the social services (see p. 117). This is largely due to the 'bias of the system' where a pluralist political order co-exists with a capitalist economy. In socialist countries, the nature of the polity and the dominant ideology is such as to subordinate the professions to lay power. No firm conclusions about the relation between the professions and the social services in socialist countries can be reached until a great deal more evidence on these questions becomes available. None the less, it seems fairly clear that the development of social policy in the U.S.S.R. has not meant a consolidation of vested professional interests. Indeed, the socialist revolution had quite the opposite effect.[90] The curb on professional autonomy has meant several things. The professions, for example the doctors, have not been in a position to safeguard the clients' interests against lay authority (e.g. the submissive role of the doctors during the forced draft industrialisation). But on the other hand there has been no 'usurpation' of the social services, in particular of medical care, by professional interests. One major consequence seems to have been that the social services are orientated more to the clients' needs and rather less to the profession's 'needs' — notice for example, the greater importance of preventive medicine in the U.S.S.R. compared to the West.[91]

We turn next to the question of bureaucratisation and alienation. How far have the social services given rise to a form of administration that results in an alienative relation between the state and the citizen? Here again we must recognise that the context in which the social services operate in socialist society is quite different from that in capitalist society. As we saw earlier, in the latter the social services operate within the confines of an economy where goods and services are generally supplied through the market. The contrast between the services provided through the market (which, to make an ideal-typical distinction, involve little officialdom and red tape, are responsive to consumer needs because of competition and entail a relation of 'equality' between the buyer and seller resulting from cash transaction) and the social services with their bureaucratism underlines the negative features of the latter. In the U.S.S.R., by contrast, the entire economy is bureaucratised. Social services are merely a part of this whole. In one sense therefore the Soviet citizen is less likely to feel deprived, for although bureaucratism may be quite pronounced, he has not got the 'reference group' of a market-provided service for comparison. On the other hand, evidence of the frustration and exasperation felt by many Soviet people with the workings of the bureaucratic administration is by no means lacking.[92] Again the nature of the service may be more important here than the social system. Thus it appears that in the U.S.S.R. as in the U.K., medicine and education are less likely to be plagued by the dysfunctions of bureaucracy than the non-professional services, e.g. income maintenance and housing.[93]

Finally the question of citizen participation in the administration of the services must be considered. On the face of it, one might be inclined to deny the existence of citizen participation altogether in Soviet society since it is ruled by a monolithic party and policy decisions are handed down from above. However, although the party rules supreme, mass participation is encouraged as it too is a part of the Marxist ideology.[94] True, participation is generally limited in scope and channeled by the party along 'correct' lines. But it would be wrong to underestimate the extent of participation by the working people, however restricted its character, in Soviet administration. In particular, the social services seem to provide a good opportunity for associating ordinary citizens as well as organisations outside the state-party apparatus with the work of administration. Thus, the trade unions play an important part in the Soviet Union in running income maintenance and assistance services and in disbursing various benefits provided by the enterprises.[95] In schools the statutory parents' committees seem to involve parents far more continuously and directly with the school than the somewhat perfunctory P.T.A.s in Britain.[96] Moreover the Soviet teachers have an obligation to keep in touch with the pupils' homes through regular visits.[97] In general it appears that the collectivist ethos of the socialist society encourages far closer links between the family and school. How far social class factors operate in the U.S.S.R. to inhibit the lower-class parents' involvement in education is difficult to tell. Class differentials in respect of participation in social and political activity do exist and higher occupational groups are, apparently, more active.[98] But it is likely that the sort of class barriers commonplace in capitalist society are absent in the U.S.S.R.

and that this is conducive to a closer identification and involvement on the part of the ordinary Soviet people with schools. In the case of housing too, Soviet tenants participate in the management of the housing estates through various residents' committees. By contrast, council housing in Britain seems to involve the tenants a good deal less.[99]

Socialist societies, such as the Soviet Union, have been described as 'mobilisational bureaucracies'. True, mass mobilisation behind particular policies is a characteristic of these societies and this entails participation. But they have also been described as having a 'participant-subject' political culture.[100] In other words, there is a great deal of participation, but of a 'guided' or 'managed' variety with the citizens in a subject status in relation to the party. Thus we have a somewhat contradictory situation. The collectivist ethos of these societies and the dominant ideology encourage involvement and participation; at the same time they cannot permit free and spontaneous participation. To complicate matters further, the situation differs from that of the Western countries in significant ways: first, the social situation in Soviet society is one of relative classlessness and second, the social services are not an adjunct to a market society – a concession as it were to certain defects of *laissez-faire* – but a 'normal' socialist institution for meeting needs. These two characteristics of socialist society suggest a far more favourable condition for a participatory and non-alienative (and in this sense 'democratic') social service. However without knowing a great deal more about the nature and extent of participation of the Soviet people and about their attitudes towards the social services, further speculation would be unprofitable.

Conclusion

This chapter has looked at the nature of welfare and its major determinants and consequences in socialist society. Each of these three aspects of welfare differs in quite fundamental ways from its counterpart in capitalist society. This is largely due to the different economic and political structures of capitalism and socialism. We have stressed the dissimilarities between the two systems because in our view they are basic.[101] However, we have also noted similarities, e.g. the work-related nature of income maintenance services, the use of charges and means tests, the effect of social services in legitimating the existing social order. Moreover, recent economic reforms in Soviet and East European societies point towards a greater use of market mechanism in the economy and wider income differentials. These economic policies cannot help affecting social policy. The situation remains somewhat unclear but in the long run their general effect may be to limit movement towards the increasing 'social' distribution decreed in Marxist ideology. This no doubt suggests a tendency towards 'convergence', namely that both Western and socialist societies may have to work with some kind of institutional welfare – a mixture of social and economic (market) distribution of goods and services. What must be recognised, however, is that similarities of this nature (and other existing similarities) are not likely to affect the basic differences in the structure of capitalist and socialist society. Behind superficial similarities, the dynamic of society and welfare relationships in the two social systems remains distinct. An adequate analysis of welfare must be based on recognising this basic structural difference between capitalism and socialism even though they share a common industrial technology and certain other elements of social organisation.

Concluding Remarks

In the course of the detailed exposition of issues and arguments, the broader themes of a book inevitably recede into the background. The concluding section offers an opportunity to redress the balance – to bring some of the broader latent themes to the surface and to develop and emphasise some of the points made earlier in the text.

A major theme of this book has been the significance of welfare as a social institution. In pursuing this theme we had to abandon the utilitarian approach which identifies social policy with government action about certain problems and services, and looks for practically relevant and 'useful' knowledge. We traced the idea of welfare through a variety of perspectives and followed its concrete expression in capitalist and socialist societies. In the course of this exploration – of the different views of welfare and its various institutional forms – the essential identity of welfare has, I hope, emerged. But this identity, like that of any other social institution, is far from simple. It is not a 'given', like an object. In seeking to understand the nature of welfare through society and welfare relationships, we have encountered a number of universal notions which are largely contradictory, for example community and conflict, stratification and integration.

Moreover these notions themselves are rich in ambiguity, and we have not probed their different meanings. Those who see social (and human) life as essentially dualistic will not be surprised to learn that social institutions encapsulate contradictory purposes, functions and sentiments. Thus the family, the site of deepest affection, loyalty and solidarity, also harbours dissension, hatred and bad faith. And if it is a haven of affection and solidarity, self-interest and 'instrumental' action also flourish within it. Religion, that most 'sacred' of institutions, is also the site of profane motives and functions. And if it integrates the believers into a community it also divides men by creating the 'out-group' of unbelievers. As with the family and religion – so it is with welfare. The objectives, motives and consequences built into the institutions of welfare show the same duality, or rather multiplicity. Social control and social integration, selfish professional or other group interests as well as altruism, efficiency as well as justice, solidarity as well as conflict have nourished and have in turn been nourished by what are known as the institutions of 'welfare'. To recognise this multiplicity is not, however, to reach the end of enquiry. On the contrary, it is rather to conclude the preliminaries, after which the 'real' business of enquiry must begin. For the nature of a specific institution of welfare in a particular society cannot be determined *a priori*. Its purposes and consequences have to be researched and established as Titmuss, for example, does so brilliantly in relation to health or as Marx does, in another context, in relation to factory legislation. Yet the preliminary investigation is important and for two reasons. One, it indicates in a generalised way the range of possibilities within which explanations may have to be sought. Second, it points to those linkages with the social structure which establish the identity of welfare as a social institution. Both the inventory of motives and consequences and the more specific connections between welfare and social structure, established through the preliminary enquiry, help to 'integrate' welfare with society. Henceforward, specific investigations and explanations of social policy lose their 'disembodied' existence and 'connect' with the social in a deeper sense. Welfare loses its 'alien' character – de-socialised, *ad hoc* and technical – and takes its rightful place alongside other institutions of society.

This book has allowed us a (brief) glance at welfare in industrial society. We have not looked at the nature of welfare in pre-industrial, e.g. agrarian and primitive, societies. However even the brief survey of capitalist and socialist societies has, I hope, demonstrated the significance of welfare in its idealistic as well as functional aspects. The ideal of a welfare society has inspired the Marxist revolutions of our time. Both the foundation of the socialist societies and a good deal of their practice since, despite many distortions and outrages, has been influenced by the conception of a welfare society. Broadly similar ideals of social relations, though in a less total form, have inspired the socialist and a good many humanitarian movements in capitalist society, movements which have helped to bring about the welfare state. Once more, however, the variety of motives and consequences must be kept in mind. Welfare, like religion or the family, can be as much an instrument of domination as of other, benign, purposes. This is no less true of socialist than of capitalist society. To say this is to draw attention to its functional aspects. For welfare may serve ends other than simply the well-being of the individuals concerned. Expediency – pure pragmatism and practicality – rather than the ideal of a good society may lie behind the practice of welfare. But whatever the motives and consequences, the importance of collective action centred around the concept of human need in modern societies cannot be doubted.

To draw attention to the growth of the institutions of welfare – especially those centred on the national community or the state, i.e. the social services – is not to claim its 'inevitability'. Yet one thing is clear. Sociological analysis suggests some very good reasons for the specific patterns of welfare in modern society, and for the importance of social regulation more generally. The greater interdependence within and between nations, the continuing use and development of industrial technology, as well as the question of the depletion of world resources suggests that *laissez-faire* is now of decreasing relevance. Indeed, it is partly because the consequences of *laissez-faire* for developed capitalism have been fraught with disaster that state intervention has become necessary. There is every reason to believe that social regulation of the economy in some form or another will be even more necessary in the future.

On the other hand the socialist countries contain a warning. The experience of the U.S.S.R. and other countries raises the question how far altruism (the recognition of the other's need before or at least equally with one's own) can in fact be institutionalised as the preponderant value in modern society. For the socialist societies show that the quest for equality and fraternity can lead to repression – to the extinguishing of freedom and individuality. Moreover it is likely that extreme egalitarianism in distribution is not conducive to efficiency and social innovation. In other words, perhaps no modern society can, in the long run, work well if it is founded on only one aspect of that duality which pervades, indeed defines, the human situation. In short, fraternity and collectivity must be balanced with liberty and individuality. Societies can be built around the pre-eminence of one or the other of these dichotomous values, but neither can be banished entirely without untoward consequences. In other words, need as well as other values, e.g. achievement, may have to be recognised and rewarded. In institutional terms this means that communal as well as market distribution of resources is likely to feature permanently in advanced societies. Indeed the market is an important human invention. And if it is seen as a tool, a social artefact that can be put to various uses, then there is no reason why it should not harmonise with public provision. For in advanced societies the choice is hardly between market and public provision. Elements of market have developed in socialist society while public provision has long become a feature of capitalist society. The question rather is which of the two will be the dominant partner and what particular values will they serve. A market and class society can be made to function more smoothly with the help of state intervention. Alternatively, market and other voluntaristic forms of social interaction can be woven into the fabric of a society whose values are need-orientated and whose economic and social activity is communally controlled. Sociological reasoning and evidence supports the judgement that the latter is preferable as the way of the future.

But this is not to deny that state collectivism gives rise to various 'dysfunctions', for example bureaucratism. Indeed this is one reason why socialist societies have begun to make greater use of the market mechanism in some respects. However, the answer to bureaucratism is not simply a return to the market just as the deficiencies of a market society do not entail the total rejection of the market mechanism as a tool. Once both market and social provision are accepted as necessary features of society, the answer to bureaucratism cannot be sought in the market place. Rather bureaucratism and alienation must be tackled as problems in their own right. There is no reason, *a priori*, why they cannot be overcome, or at least their effects minimised, through appropriate institutional changes. However, as we have seen earlier, in differing ways both capitalist and socialist (present-day) societies remain resistant to these changes.

Finally we would like to draw attention to an issue on which two leading social philosophers of our time, Richard Titmuss and Ivan Illich,[1] converge. In their different ways they have reminded us that the social services are not necessarily humane institutions, structured to satisfy human needs. As Titmuss wrote, especially in connection with the health services, 'needs' can be developed 'artificially' by those – the professionals and administrators – who man the social services.[2] If the social services develop on the basis of such partisan definition of needs they are more likely to benefit those who run them than the clients themselves. This insight, a warning note sounded by Titmuss soon after the founding of the post-war British welfare state, has of course been dramatised on a much wider canvas by Ivan Illich. Illich has made out a strong case for the dehumanising potential of professionally defined and administered services such as education and medical care.[3] Whatever the exaggerations in Illich's argument, its basic truth cannot be questioned. No doctor or teacher reflecting in private (public utterances are quite another matter) will find it easy to decide whether the basic assumptions underlying the service he provides (or the research he does) have more to do with professional or client interests. Illich's solutions may be far too radical, and unrelated to the social structure as a whole, to appear realistic. But there is little doubt that he has drawn our attention forcefully to an important dysfunction of present-day social services (indeed of services such as education and health care in modern societies generally – whether private or publicly provided). Illich's argument, concerned largely with professional and commercial vested interests, is particularly true of capitalist society. But as he points out, it is also relevant for socialist societies,[4] whose ideas of development and progress have been heavily influenced by the capitalist West. In short the negative implications of professionalism for the social services, a theme merely touched on in passing by Titmuss, find fuller, if somewhat extreme, expression in Illich's works.

Illich has also stressed the role of technology in creating 'diswelfare'. Titmuss – indeed the tradition of social administration generally – has not been critical of technology as such. This is understandable. The 'realistic' school of West European socialism (social-democratic as well as Marxist) and reformist thinking generally has seen the development of industrial technology largely as progress. Technology has been viewed as a neutral tool whose consequences flow from the kind of socio-political system it serves. It has been left to Illich, among others, to argue that types of technology, to some extent independent of the social system within which they exist, can have consequences inimical to a humane social order.[5] In particular, the logic of professional and scientific development can lead to 'spectacular' technologies (e.g. in curative medicine) which, apart from increasing the dependence of the client on the expert, may further professional and scientific interests far more than those of the client. This critique of technology, which to some extent cuts across capitalist and socialist systems, has important policy implications not only for medical care but also for education, transport and certain other services.

These and other weaknesses of the social services as a model of humane social organisation have received scant attention in the literature of social administration. The reasons for this are many, an obvious one being that in capitalist society social administration is largely preoccupied with fighting a defensive battle against *laissez-faire*. This indirect definition of its subject matter by the dominant social principle of capitalism seems to have left little room for a wider perspective. The exploration of the society-welfare relationship, however, suggests the need for a close examination of such areas as professionalism, the prospects for preventive social policies, the implications of medical and other scientific and technological developments for social provision.

Finally, it should perhaps be made clear that the approach adopted in this book (which may be described as 'sociology of welfare') is not meant as an alternative to social administration. Its aim is rather to complement, hopefully to enrich, the subject matter of social administration. A main objective of the book was to prepare the theoretical groundwork for the study of welfare as a social phenomenon. How far it may have succeeded in this is a question that can only be answered by the reader. In any case, if it stimulates some sociologists' interest in the subject matter of social administration and encourages some students of social administration to look at their subject matter in its wider societal context, our endeavour will have been worthwhile.

Notes and References

Chapter One

1. Robert Pinker, *Social Theory and Social Policy* (London: Heinemann, 1971) p. xii.
2. Ibid., p. 49.
3. Ibid., p. 50.
4. See Brian Abel-Smith, 'Richard Morris Titmuss' (obituary notice) in *Journal of Social Policy*, vol. 2(2), Apr 1973.
5. D. V. Donnison *et al.*, *Social Policy and Administration* (London: Allen and Unwin, 1965) ch. 2; Joyce Warham, 'Social Administration and Sociology', *Journal of Social Policy*, vol. 2(3), Jul 1973; Maurice Broady, *Social Administration: Some Current Concerns*, inaugural lecture, University College of Swansea, 1972.
6. Pinker, *Social Theory and Social Policy*, p. 48n.
7. 'The Social Division of Welfare' in Richard M. Titmuss, *Essays on the Welfare State* (London: Allen and Unwin, 1963).
8. Donnison *et al. Social Policy and Administration*, p. 26 and Donnison, 'Social Administration Evolves', *New Society*, (20 Oct 1966).
9. Karl R. Popper, *Conjectures and Refutations: The Growth of Scientific Knowledge* (London: Routledge, 1963).
10. Broady, *Social Administration: Some Current Concerns*, p. 6.
11. Pinker, *Social Theory and Social Policy*, p. xi.
12. Dorothy Wedderburn, 'Facts and Theories of the Welfare State' in *The Socialist Register 1965*, ed. Ralph Miliband and John Saville (London: Merlin, 1965), p. 128.
13. Thus in 1898 New Zealand became the first English-speaking country to introduce non-contributory old age pensions (ten years

earlier than Britain) and in 1926 the first in the world to grant family allowances. Both benefits were means tested. See P. R. Kaim-Caudle, *Comparative Social Policy and Social Security* (London: Martin Robertson, 1973) pp. 156, 251.

14. The Social Security Act of 1938 introduced what amounted to a free and universal health service. See W. B. Sutch, *The Quest for Security in New Zealand* (London: Oxford University Press, 1966) pp. 243–8. The post-war governments however seem to have encouraged private rather than socialised medicine. See Kaim-Caudle, *Comparative Social Policy and Social Security*, p. 323.

15. 'War and Social Policy' in Titmuss, *Essays on the Welfare State.*

16. 'Trends in Social Policy: Health', Richard M. Titmuss, *Commitment to Welfare* (London: Allen and Unwin, 1968).

17. Ibid., pp. 238, 241.

18. Although British 'socialised medicine' has been the subject of investigation by many American scholars I am not aware of any systematic comparison of the development of health care in the two countries. But see Brian Abel-Smith, 'The History of Medical Care', *Comparative Development in Social Welfare*, ed. E. W. Martin (London: Allen and Unwin, 1972). For a more general comparison of the development of welfare in Europe and America see Arnold J. Heidenheimer, 'The Politics of Public Education, Health and Welfare in U.S.A. and Western Europe: How Growth and Reform Potentials have Differed', *British Journal of Political Science*, vol. 3(3), Jul 1973.

19. Pinker, *Social Theory and Social Policy*, p. 12.

20. Ibid., p. 130.

21. Ibid., pp. 98–9, 106–7, 130.

22. Peter Bachrach and Morton S. Baratz, *Power and Poverty. Theory and Practice* (New York: Oxford University Press, 1970).

23. J. H. Westergaard 'Sociology: the Myth of Classlessness' in *Ideology in Social Science*, ed. Robin Blackburn (Fontana, 1972), p. 155.

24. Ibid., p. 156.

25. Richard M. Titmuss, *The Gift Relationship* (London: Allen and Unwin, 1970).

26. Ibid., pp. 220–21, 271–2.

27. Ibid., p. 235.

28. Ibid., p. 253.

29. Ibid.

30. Ibid., p. 255.

31. Ibid., p. 252.

32. Donnison *et al.*, *Social Policy and Administration*, p. 23.

33. Titmuss, *The Gift Relationship*, p. 272. Both the title and content of his Fabian lecture 'The Irresponsible Society' is very revealing in this respect; his critique of the post-war capitalist society in Britain is basically moral rather than structural. See *Essays on the Welfare State*, ch. 11.

34. Donnison *et al.*, *Social Policy and Administration*, p. 26.

35. 'The Subject of Social Administration', Richard M. Titmuss, *Commitment to Welfare*, p. 23.

36. Warham, *Journal of Social Policy*, 2(3).

37. Ibid., p. 207.

Chapter Two

1. 'Citizenship and Social Class', first published in 1950, is included in T. H. Marshall, *Sociology at the Crossroads and Other Essays* (London: Heinemann, 1963).

2. Ibid., pp. 67–9.

3. See for example Talcott Parsons, *The System of Modern Societies* (New Jersey: Prentice-Hall, 1971); Reinhard Bendix, *Nation-Building and Citizenship* (New York: John Wiley, 1964); Gerhard Lenski, *Power and Privilege,* New York: McGraw-Hill, 1966).

4. Marshall, *Sociology at the Crossroads*, p. 74.

5. Of the many concepts of contrasting social order formulated in the nineteenth century, Tönnies' *Gemeinschaft* (community) and *Gesellschaft* (association) is one of the best known. See for example Robert A. Nisbet, *The Sociological Tradition* (London: Heinemann, 1967) pp. 71–82; Peter Worsley and others, *Introducing Sociology* (Harmondsworth: Penguin, 1970) ch. 6.

6. Marshall, *Sociology at the Crossroads*, p. 96.

7. Ibid., pp. 72–3, 87, 90, 107, 122.

8. Dorothy Wedderburn. 'Facts and Theories of the Welfare State' in *The Socialist Register 1965*, ed. Ralph Miliband and John Saville (London: Merlin, 1965) p. 139.

9. Marshall, *Sociology at the Crossroads*, p. 107.

10. Ibid., p. 91.

11. Ibid., p. 122.

12. Parsons, *The System of Modern Societies*, pp. 20–22, 92–4. See also 'Full Citizenship for the Negro American?', Talcott Parsons, *Sociological Theory and Modern Society* (New York; The Free Press, 1967).

13. Marshall, *Sociology at the Crossroads*, p. 86.

14. Ibid.

15. Ibid., p. 75.

16. A. V. Dicey, *Law and Public Opinion in England* (London: Macmillan, 1962).

17. Marshall, *Sociology at the Crossroads*, pp. 81–6.

18. This was recognised by Marshall later. See his 'The Welfare State and the Affluent Society' in *Sociology at the Crossroads*.

19. Ibid., p. 74.

20. The American Constitution itself may be taken as having established civil rights. As to political rights, by mid-nineteenth century adult (white) manhood suffrage had become established throughout the states. After the Civil War, the 14th and 15th amendments extended these rights to the blacks although they ceased to be effective in the Southern states.

21. While free public education for all became established by mid-nineteenth century, it was not until the 1930s that the social rights of income maintenance made a start. Housing and medical care have yet to be recognised as social rights.

22. Bismarck's social insurance legislation was passed after the suppression of political rights (albeit for the socialists only). While the German state did a good deal to improve and extend social benefits during the years before the First World War, neither political nor industrial democracy made any headway. See Koppel S. Pinson, *Modern Germany* (London: Macmillan, 1966) pp. 156–60, 245–6; John H. Herz, *The Government of Germany* (New York: Harcourt Brace, 1972) pp. 45–6.

23. Marshall, *Sociology at the Crossroads*, pp. 81–3, 90.

24. Ibid., p. 90.

25. Ibid.

26. Ibid., p. 97.

27. Ibid., p. 86.

28. Ibid., p. 97.

29. On Marx see ch. 5 and on Spencer and Durkheim ch. 4 below. See also Robert Pinker, *Social Theory and Social Policy* (London: Heinemann: 1971) ch. 1.

30. See p. 45–6 below.

31. Julia Parker, *Social Policy and Citizenship* (London: Macmillan, 1975) p. 41.

32. Pinker, *Social Theory and Social Policy*, pp. 200–201.

33. Parker, *Social Policy and Citizenship*, p. 146.

34. Pinker, *Social Theory and Social Policy*, p. 201.

35. Marshall, *Sociology at the Crossroads*, p. 122.

36. Thus Asa Briggs finds that 'in the light of recent statistical studies of continuing deprivation' Marshall's thesis 'looks far too stilted', and believes that it 'would now need not a supplement but a revision'. See E. W. Martin (ed.), *Comparative Development in Social Welfare* (London: Allen and Unwin, 1972) pp. 20–21.

Chapter Three

1. In some form or another the notion of similarity or increasing similarity of the social structure of industrial societies is to be found in the work of many post-war sociologists and economists. Two best known works are Clark Kerr and others, *Industrialism and Industrial Man* (Harmondsworth: Penguin, 1973) and J. K. Galbraith, *The New Industrial State* (London: Hamish Hamilton, 1967). I have chosen to focus on the Kerr version of the theory which is a comprehensive sociological presentation of the thesis.

2. Galbraith, ibid., p. 396.

3. See, for example Harold L. Wilensky and Charles N. Lebeaux, *Industrial Society and Social Welfare* (New York: Free Press, 1965).

4. Kerr, *Industrialism and Industrial Man*, ch. 2.

5. Ibid., pp. 61–4, 193.

6. Ibid., pp. 65–7, 196. The authors stress the role of the enterprise rather than the state but their argument is equally valid for state paternalism.

7. Ibid., pp. 70–73, 195–8.

8. Ibid., p. 270.

9. Ibid.

10. Ibid., p. 186.

11. Ibid., p. 73 and ch. 8 *passim.*

12. For a general critique of the theoretical arguments underlying convergence thesis see J. H. Goldthorpe, 'Social Stratification in Industrial Society'; *The Development of Industrial Societies: Sociological Review Monograph No. 8.* (Keele: University of Keele, 1964) and Reinhard John Skinner, 'Technological Determinism: A Critique of Convergence Theory', *Comparative Studies in Society and History*, vol. 18(1), Jan 1976.

13. See Ramesh Mishra, 'Welfare and Industrial Man', *Sociological Review*, NS vol. 21(4), Nov 1973 and 'Convergence Theory and Social Change: The Development of Welfare in Britain and the Soviet Union' *Comparative Studies in Society and History*, vol. 18(1), Jan 1976.

14. See p. 97 below.

15. Richard M. Titmuss, *The Gift Relationship* (Harmondsworth: Penguin, 1973) esp. ch. 10.

16. John H. Goldthorpe, 'The Development of Social Policy in England, 1800–1914', *Transactions of the Fifth World Congress of Sociology*, vol. 4 (1962) p. 56. It is true to say, however, that once the group-action type of account is brought into the picture, the result can not be a mere supplementation but in some ways a revision of the theory. For a 'phenomenological' critique of explanations of social policy development see John Carrier and Ian Kendall, 'Social Policy and Social Change', *Journal of Social Policy*, vol. 2(3), July 1973.

Chapter Four

1. Percy S. Cohen, *Modern Social Theory* (London: Heinemann, 1968) pp. 34–7.

2. Robert Pinker, *Social Theory and Social Policy* (London: Heinemann, 1971) ch. 1.

3. Donald Macrae (ed.), *Spencer: The Man Versus the State* (Harmondsworth: Penguin, 1969) Introduction, pp. 14–17, 27, 35; see also J. D. Y. Peel, *Herbert Spencer* (London: Heinemann, 1971).

4. Pinker, *Social Theory and Social Policy*, pp. 26–9.

5. Emile Durkheim, *The Division of Labor in Society* (New York: Free Press, 1964), p. 221.

6. Ibid., p. 222.

7. Ibid., p. 227.

8. Ibid.
9. Ibid., p. 197.
10. Ibid., p. 28.
11. Pinker, *Social Theory and Social Policy*, pp. 17–18.
12. Durkheim, *Division of Labor in Society*, pp. 24, 26–8.
13. Talcott Parsons, *The Social System* (London: Routledge, 1951); Robert K. Merton, *Social Theory and Social Structure* (New York: Free Press, 1968); Neil J. Smelser, *Social Change in the Industrial Revolution* (London: Routledge, 1959) are among the leading works of these writers.
14. See for example Talcott Parsons and Neil J. Smelser, *Economy and Society* (London: Routledge, 1956) pp. 18–19.
15. This distinction, implicit in functional analysis, has in fact been spelled out by a neo-Marxist, David Lockwood. See his 'Social Integration and System Integration' in *Explorations in Social Change*, ed. George K. Zollschan and Walter Hirsch (London: Routledge, 1964).
16. Neil J. Smelser, 'Toward a Theory of Modernization' in *Social Change*, ed. Amitai Etzioni and Eva Etzioni (New York: Basic Books, 1964).
17. Ibid., p. 261.
18. Ibid., p. 267.
19. Ibid., p. 268.
20. Raymond Firth, *Human Types* (New York: Mentor, 1958) ch. III; Marshall Sahlins, *Stone Age Economics* (London; Tavistock, 1974) chs. 1 and 5; Gerhard E. Lenski, *Power and Privilege* (New York: McGraw-Hill, 1966) chs. 5 and 6.
21. Weber notes this role of religion though not necessarily from a functionlist standpoint. See Max Weber, *The Sociology of Religion* (London: Methuen, 1965) pp. 210–15. See also Lenski, *Power and Privilege*, pp. 263–6. For the 'anti-welfare' attitudes of individualistic religions such as puritanism see R. H. Tawney, *Religion and the Rise of Capitalism* (Harmondsworth: Penguin, 1969) pp. 251–70.
22. Richard M. Titmuss, *Commitment to Welfare* (London: Allen and Unwin, 1968) p. 22.
23. Michael Young and Peter Willmott, *Family and Kinship in East London* (London: Routledge, 1957).
24. Merton, *Social Theory and Social Structure*, pp. 80–81, 105.
25. Ibid.

26. Ibid., p. 105.

27. Max Weber, *The Protestant Ethic and the Spirit of Capitalism* (London: Allen and Unwin, 1968).

28. See for example Richard M. Titmuss, *Essays on the Welfare State* (London: Allen and Unwin, 1963) pp. 24–7.

29. Merton, *Social Theory and Social Structure*, p. 106.

30. Peter Townsend, *Sociology and Social Policy* (London: Allen Lane, Penguin, 1975) p. 2.

31. Titmuss, *Essays on the Welfare State*, ch. 2.

32. See Neil J. Smelser 'Toward a Theory of Modernization' in Etzioni and Etzioni (eds) op. cit. Peter Townsend's mordant critique of functionalist analysis of change seems to overlook this point about re-integration. See Townsend, op. cit., pp. 14–16.

33. Smelser, in *Social Change*, p. 268.

34. See Sidney and Beatrice Webb, *English Poor Law History: Part II, Vol. I* (London: Frank Cass, 1963).

35. Kingsley Davis and Wilbert E. Moore, 'Some Principles of Stratification' in *Class, Status, and Power*, ed. Reinhard Bendix and Seymour Martin Lipset (London: Routledge, 1967).

36. Emile Durkheim, *Suicide* (London: Routledge, 1972) pp. 254–7.

37. John Horton, 'The Dehumanization of Anomie and Alienation', *British Journal of Sociology*, vol. 15(4), Dec 1964, p. 286.

38. Parsons, who fully recognises the role of social rights (see p. 23 above) in the formation of the societal community of the modern nation-state, none the less fails to note the relevance of the welfare state for the problem of anomie. No doubt this is because Parsons and other functionalists stress the normative (moral) aspects of anomie and totally ignore its factual dimensions.

39. See for example Neil J. Smelser, *The Sociology of Economic Life* (Englewood Cliffs: Prentice-Hall, 1963) pp. 88, 108.

40. Typical of the functionalist approach is to assume that the family is already being helped in this way! See Smelser, *The Sociology of Economic Life*, p. 88.

41. Alvin W. Gouldner, *The Coming Crisis of Western Sociology* (London: Heinemann, 1971) p. 342.

42. Ibid., pp. 344–51.

Chapter Five

1. This chapter, especially the section on Marx, draws heavily on Ramesh Mishra, 'Marx and Welfare', *Sociological Review*, NS vol. 23(2), May 1975.

2. Robert Pinker, *Social Theory and Social Policy* (London: Heinemann, 1971) pp. 32–3.

3. See Mishra, *Sociological Review*, for relevant sources.

4. This paragraph is based on K. Marx and F. Engels, 'Communist Manifesto' and K. Marx 'A Contribution to the Critique of Political Economy (Preface)'. See Lewis S. Feuer (ed.), *Marx and Engels: Basic Writings* (London: Fontana, 1969), chs. I and II.

5. See 'Communist Manifesto' and K. Marx and F. Engels, *The German Ideology*, Part One (London: Lawrence and Wishart, 1974).

6. See 'Communist Manifesto', and 'Economic and Philosophical Manuscripts' in T. B. Bottomore, *Karl Marx: Early Writings* (London: Watts, 1963).

7. See 'Economic and Philosophical Manuscripts' in Bottomore, *Karl Marx* and *The German Ideology*.

8. See for example 'Inaugural Address of the Working Men's International Association' in K. Marx and F. Engels, *On Britain* (Moscow: Foreign Languages Publishing House, 1962).

9. For Marx's scepticism about factory legislation see for example, K. Marx, *Capital*, vol. I (London: Lawrence and Wishart, 1974) pp. 377, 451–65 *passim*.

10. Ibid., pp. 20, 264–86 *passim*.

11. Ibid., pp. 279–80, 283.

12. 'Inaugural Address', p. 489.

13. See for example 'Communist Manifesto' in Feuer (ed.), *Marx and Engels*, pp. 51, 70.

14. *Capital*, vol. I, p. 464.

15. Ibid., pp. 264–6, 269, 464.

16. Ibid., pp. 603–4, 611–7, 624.

17. Mishra, *Sociological Review*, pp. 298–9.

18. See for example Robin Blackburn, 'The Unequal Society' in *Power in Britain*, ed. John Urry and John Wakeford (London: Heinemann, 1973); Ian Gough, 'State Expenditure in Advanced Capitalism', *New Left Review*, vol. 92, Jul-Aug 1975; Paul A. Baran and Paul M. Sweezy, *Monopoly Capital: An Essay on the American*

Economic and Social Order (Harmondsworth: Penguin, 1968) chs. 6 and 10.

19. John Saville. 'The Welfare State: An Historical Approach', *New Reasoner* 3, 1957–8.

20. Ibid., p. 6.

21. Ibid., p. 8.

22. G. W. Domhoff, *The Higher Circles: The Governing Class in America* (New York: Random House, 1971).

23. Ibid., pp. 156–8, 184–6.

24. Ibid., p. 197.

25. See for example Saville, *New Reasoner*, p. 22.

26. Ibid., p. 24.

27. Domhoff, *The Higher Circles*, p. 217.

28. Ibid., p. 218.

29. Saville, *New Reasoner*, p. 24.

30. Ibid.

31. Ernest Mandel, *Marxist Economic Theory* (London: Merlin, 1968).

32. Ibid., p. 530.

33. Ibid., pp. 337, 533.

34. See n. 18.

35. Baran and Sweezy, *Monopoly Capital*, ch. 6.

36. Mandel, *Marxist Economic Theory*, p. 498.

37. Ibid. pp. 498–9; Ralph Miliband, *The State in Capitalist Society* (London: Quartet Books, 1973) ch. 4 *passim*.

38. Mandel, *Marxist Economic Theory*, p. 501.

39. Frances Fox Piven and Richard A. Cloward's *Regulating the Poor: The Functions of Public Welfare* (London: Tavistock, 1972) seeks to demonstrate this in respect of public assistance (poor relief).

40. See Gaston V. Rimlinger, *Welfare Policy and Industrialization in Europe, America, and Russia* (New York: John Wiley, 1971) pp. 111–14, 130.

41. Ibid., pp. 117–21.

42. Quoted in Ralph Miliband, *Parliamentary Socialism* (London: Merlin, 1973), p. 37n.

43. Bernard Semmel, *Imperialism and Social Reform* (London: Allen and Unwin, 1960); Bentley B. Gilbert, *The Evolution of National Insurance in Great Britain* (London: Michael Joseph, 1966) ch. 2.

44. See G. R. Searle, *The Quest for National Efficiency* (Oxford: Blackwell, 1971).

45. Semmel, *Imperialism and Social Reform*, ch. 2.

46. Mandel, *Marxist Economic Theory*, p. 533.

47. Ibid., p. 338.

48. Baran and Sweezy, *Monopoly Capital*, p. 163.

49. Ibid., pp. 165–9.

50. Ibid., pp. 152–3, 156–67.

51. Mandel, *Marxist Economic Theory*, pp. 536–9. See also Miliband, *The State in Capitalist Society* ch. 9 ('Reform and Repression').

52. 'The Social Division of Welfare', Richard M. Titmuss, *Essays on the Welfare State* (London: Allen and Unwin, 1963).

53. Richard M. Titmuss, *Income Distribution and Social Change.* (London: Allen and Unwin, 1962).

54. Pinker, *Social Theory and Social Policy*, pp. 146–50.

55. Peter Townsend, *Sociology and Social Policy* (London: Allen Lane, 1975) pp. 2–6.

56. See for example, Maurice Bruce. *The Coming of the Welfare State* (London: Batsford, 1965) pp. 174–81.

57. Ramesh Mishra, 'Convergence Theory and Social Change: The Development of Welfare in Britain and the Soviet Union', *Comparative Studies in Society and History*, vol. 18(1), Jan 1976.

58. See for example Townsend, *Sociology and Social Policy*, Preface; Vic George and Paul Wilding, *Ideology and Social Welfare* (London: Routledge, 1976) ch. 6; Richard Titmuss 'Poverty versus Inequality' in *Poverty*, ed. Jack L. Roach and Janet K. Roach (Harmondsworth: Penguin, 1972); Pamela Roby (ed.), *The Poverty Establishment* (Englewood Cliffs: Prentice-Hall, 1974).

59. See Blackburn, in *Power in Britain*; J. L. Nicholson, *Redistribution of Income in the United Kingdom* (London: Bowes and Bowes, 1964) pp. 60–1 for a comparison of income distribution before and after the Second World War; Gabriel Kolko, *Wealth and Power in America* (London: Thames and Hudson, 1962) esp. ch. 2.

60. See pp. 109–14, below.

61. This point and the weakness of Marxist functional explanations of the welfare state more generally are raised by Gough, *New Left Review*, pp. 55–7, 76.

62. See for example Richard M. Titmuss 'Trends in Social Policy: Health' in his *Commitment to Welfare* (London: Allen and Unwin,

1968); A. J. Willcocks, *The Creation of the National Health Service.*
(London: Routledge, 1967); Bentley B. Gilbert, *The Evolution of*
National Insurance in Great Britain (London: Michael Joseph, 1966)
which however makes some effort to situate the specific developments
within a wider structural framework.

63. Japan and the U.S.A. See pp. 94, 105 below.

64. See Mishra, in *Sociological Review*, p. 307.

65. This is discussed in John H. Goldthorpe, 'The Development of
Social Policy in England, 1800–1914', *Transactions of the Fifth*
World Congress of Sociology, vol. 4, 1962, pp. 42–3.

66. See for example Marx and Engels, 'Communist Manifesto' in
Feuer (ed.), *Marx and Engels*, p. 81.

67. See for example Mandel, *Marxist Economic Theory*, pp.
530–4; Miliband, *The State in Capitalist Society*, pp. 72, 99.

Chapter Six

1. See Harold L. Wilensky and Charles N. Lebaux, *Industrial*
Society and Social Welfare (New York: The Free Press, 1965) pp.
138–40; Robert Pinker, *Social Theory and Social Policy* (London:
Heinemann, 1971) pp. 90–100.

2. See Ramesh Mishra, 'Welfare and Industrial Man', *Sociological*
Review, NS vol. 21(4), Nov 1973.

3. See Ramesh Mishra, 'Convergence Theory and Social Change:
The Development of Welfare in Britain and the Soviet Union', *Com-*
parative Studies in Society and History, vol. 18(1), Jan 1976, p. 36, n.
19.

4. Hugh Heclo, *Modern Social Politics in Britain and Sweden*
(New Haven: Yale University Press, 1974) p. 157.

5. See Mishra, *Comparative Studies in Society & History*, p. 43
and David Owen, *English Philanthropy 1660–1960* (Cambridge,
Mass: Harvard University Press, 1964), Part Four.

6. See G. L. Reid and D. J. Robertson (eds), *Fringe Benefits,*
Labour Costs and Social Security (London: Allen and Unwin, 1965)
for developments in Britain and the United States.

7. See for example Richard M. Titmuss, *Essays on the Welfare*
State (London: Allen and Unwin, 1963) ch. 2 and *Income Distribu-*
tion and Social Change (London: Allen and Unwin, 1962) especially
chs. 6 and 7 and Appendix D and E.

8. See for example David Horowitz and David Kolodney, 'The Foundations: Charity Begins at Home' in *The Poverty Establishment*, ed. Pamela Roby (Englewood Cliffs: Prentice-Hall, 1974).

9. Six years' schooling had become compulsory and virtually free in Japan before the First World War. In the United States free elementary education had become established by 1860 although compulsory attendance laws were not passed by all states until 1918. See *World Survey of Education Vol. II: Primary Education* (Paris: Unesco, 1958) pp. 628, 1241–2.

10. See Mishra, *Sociological Review*, pp. 550.

11. See U.S. Dept. of Health, Education and Welfare, *Social Security Programs Throughout the World, 1971* (Washington D.C.: U.S. Govt. Printing Office, 1972), pp. 110–1, 232–3. In Israel the powerful labour federation Histradut provides comprehensive health care on a voluntary basis.

12. See for example P. R. Kaim-Caudle, *Comparative Social Policy* (London: Martin Robertson, 1973), pp. 313–24.

13. The twenty countries were those with a *per capita* income equal to or greater than Japan. See Mishra, *Sociological Review*, pp. 537 and 541, and p. 558 (n. 22) for details of the eight income security risks.

14. See for example Harold L. Wilensky, *The Welfare State and Equality* (Los Angeles: University of California Press, 1975) pp. 3–7; D. V. Donnison, *The Government of Housing* (Harmondsworth: Penguin, 1967) pp. 93–4, 97.

15. J. S. Fuerst (ed.), *Public Housing in Europe and America* (London: Croom Helm, 1974) p. 18.

16. Ibid., pp. 134, 178.

17. Ibid., pp. 14–17, 192.

18. See Mishra, *Sociological Review*, pp. 543, 553, 560.

19. See Shizuo Matsushima, 'Labour Management Relations in Japan', in *Japanese Sociological Studies: The Sociological Review Monograph No. 10*, ed. Paul Halmos (University of Keele, 1966); James C. Abegglen, *The Japanese Factory* (Bombay: Asia Publishing House, 1959).

20. Abegglen, ibid., p. 35.

21. Johannes Hirschmeier and Tsunehiko Yui, *The Development of Japanese Business 1600–1973* (London: Allen and Unwin, 1975), p. 290.

22. Ibid., pp. 285–8. See also William A. Robson, *Welfare State and Welfare Society* (London: Allen and Unwin, 1976), p. 92.

23. Reid and Robertson, *Fringe Benefits*, pp. 128–31; Merton C. Bernstein, 'Private Pensions in the United States', *Journal of Social Policy*, vol. 2(1), Jan 1973.

24. Reid and Robertson, ibid., pp. 24, 29–31 and ch. 7; Heclo, *Modern Social Politics in Britain and Sweden*, p. 275. Where state schemes were more adequate (e.g. West Germany) or where social democratic influence was stronger (e.g. Sweden) occupational pensions are far less developed. See Thomas Wilson (ed.), *Pensions, Inflation and Growth* (London: Heinemann, 1974) pp. 69–71 for West Germany and Heclo, ibid., ch. 5 *passim* for Sweden.

25. Dorothy Wedderburn and Christine Craig, 'Relative Deprivation in Work' in *Poverty, Inequality and Class Structure*, ed. Dorothy Wedderburn (London: Cambridge University Press, 1974).

26. While one must be cautious in generalising about the nature of the relationship between type of industry, size of firm, fringe benefits and low pay there is little doubt that the low paid are worse off in terms of occupational benefits. On these points see Frank Field (ed.), *Low Pay* (London: Action Society Trust, 1973) pp. 24–7, 41–2, 46 and ch. 5; Reid and Robertson, *Fringe Benefits*, ch. 3; A. F. Young and J. H. Smith 'Fringe Benefits – A Local Survey', *British Journal of Industrial Relations*, vol. 5(1), Mar 1967.

27. See Seymour Broadbridge, *Industrial Dualism in Japan* (London: Frank Cass, 1966) pp. 50–2, 77; William W. Lockwood (ed.), *The State and Economic Enterprise in Japan* (Princeton, N. J.: Princeton University Press, 1965) p. 661.

28. Hirschmeier and Yui, *Development of Japanese Business*, p. 287.

29. Heclo, *Modern Social Politics in Britain and Sweden*, pp. 228–53 *passim*.

30. Ibid., pp. 156–7; Reid and Robertson, *Fringe Benefits*, p. 170; Wilson, *Pensions, Inflation and Growth*, pp. 68, 256, 306.

31. Evidence on class differentials in the provision of fringe benefits in the public sector as a whole as rather patchy. On pensions see *Occupational Pension Schemes 1971*, Fourth Survey by the Government Actuary (London: H.M.S.O., 1972); Gerald Rhodes, *Public Sector Pensions* (London: Allen and Unwin, 1965) pp. 65, 70–1, 245. On sick pay see Roy Lewis and Geoff Latta, 'Compensation for Industrial

Injury and Disease', *Journal of Social Policy* vol. 4(1), Jan 1975, p. 29. Thus in the National Coal Board the white collar workers have no qualifying period for entitlement to sick pay and are allowed six months at full pay and another six at half-pay. By contrast, miners must have one year's service for entitlement, the first seven days of each absence are unpaid, the maximum entitlement of 20 weeks at full rate is reached only after 10 years' service and the 'full rate' is only a proportion of the weekly wage (ibid.). See however Richard Pryke, *Public Enterprise in Practice* (London: McGibbon and Kee, 1971) pp. 99–100 for public sector's superiority over private in the provision of fringe benefits for manual workers.

32. See for example Kaim-Caudle, *Comparative Social Policy*, p. 250 and ch. VIII *passim*.

33. Titmuss, *Essays on the Welfare State*, p. 46.

34. J. C. Kincaid, *Poverty and Equality in Britain* (Harmondsworth: Penguin, 1973) pp. 124–5. The Labour Government is committed to replacing the present, dual, system of family and child tax allowances with a single allowance that would include payments in respect of the first child. A similar reform has already been carried out in West Germany.

35. Ibid., p. 126.

36. A ceiling of £25,000 was imposed in 1974. See the *Guardian*, 27 March 1974.

37. Titmuss, *Income Distribution and Social Change*, p. 167.

38. Kincaid, *Poverty and Equality in Britain*, p. 149.

39. Ibid., p. 150.

40. Michael Meacher, 'The Coming Class Struggle', *New Statesman*, 4 January 1974, p. 7.

41. Titmuss, *Essays on the Welfare State*, ch. 2.

42. Ibid., p. 44.

43. See for example Wilensky, *The Welfare State and Equality*, pp. 24–6; Ernest W. Burgess (ed.), *Aging in Western Societies* (Chicago University Press, 1960), ch. II.

44. See n. 9 above.

45. See W. W. Rostow, *British Economy of the Nineteenth Century* (London: Oxford University Press, 1966); Philip S. Bagwell and G. E. Mingay, *Britain and America 1850–1939* (London: Routledge, 1970) ch. 10; G. P. Jones and A. G. Pool, *A Hundred Years of Economic Development in Great Britain (1840–1940)* (London:

Duckworth, 1959) pp. 199–204, 299–305.

46. See for example Donald Winch, *Economics and Policy* (London: Collins/Fontana, 1972) Part Two.

47. See for example W. B. Sutch, *The Quest for Security in New Zealand 1840 to 1966* (London: Oxford University Press, 1966) esp. chs. 9–13; Larry Hufford, *Sweden: the Myth of Socialism* (London: Fabian Society, 1973) pp. 2–3, 9, 19–20; Peter Townsend and Nicholas Bosanquet (eds), *Labour and Inequality* (London: Fabian Society, 1972) p. 6.

48. This is a hypothesis that needs to be tested against cross-national evidence. But we could cite at least one statistical study in support of our thesis. See Frederic L. Pryor, *Public Expenditures in Communist and Capitalist Nations* (London: Allen and Unwin, 1968) pp. 172–3, 473–5 for the association between unionisation of the work force and the development of old age pensions before the First World War.

49. See Gaston V. Rimlinger, *Welfare Policy and Industrialisation in Europe, America, and Russia* (New York: John Wiley, 1971) chs. 4 and 7; Gordon Hyde, *The Soviet Health Service* (London: Lawrence and Wishart, 1974) ch. 1 for health services before the revolution.

50. See Anthony King 'Ideas, Institutions and the Policies of Governments: a Comparative Analysis', *British Journal of Political Science*, vol. 3(3), Jul 1973, p. 309 for the extent of state collectivism in Germany before the First World War.

51. In 1911 state expenditure accounted for less than 7 per cent of the total. See W. Harbutt Dawson, *Social Insurance in Germany 1883–1911* (London: Unwin, 1912) pp. 236–7.

52. Ibid., p. 257.

53. For the statistics of labour force unionised in Britain and the United States see Philip S. Bagwell and G. E. Mingay, *Britain and America 1850–1939; A Study of Economic Change* (London: Routledge, 1970) p. 207. For more recent European and American figures see Allan G. Gruchy, *Comparative Economic Systems* (Boston: Houghton Mifflin, 1966) p. 313.

54. See for example Seymour Martin Lipset, *The First New Nation* (London: Heinemann, 1964) esp. ch. 5.

55. See for example Wilensky, *The Welfare State and Equality*, pp. 34–5, 37–9.

56. Rimlinger, *Welfare Policy and Industrialisation*, pp. 240–3;

Reid and Robertson, *Fringe Benefits*, pp. 129–30; Arnold J. Heidenheimer, 'The Politics of Public Education, Health and Welfare in the U.S.A. and Western Europe', *British Journal of Political Science*, vol. 3(3), Jul 1973, pp. 323–4, 332–3.

57. Rimlinger, ibid., pp. 80–5; J. David Greenstone, *Labor in American Politics*, (New York: Random House, 1970), p. 26.

58. Greenstone, ibid., pp. 23–4.

59. See for example Sidney and Beatrice Webb, *The History of Trade Unionism*, (London: Longmans Green, 1920) ch. VII and B. C. Roberts, *The Trades Union Congress 1868–1921* (London: Allen and Unwin, 1958) pp. 96–7, 127–9 for the *laissez-faire* values and attitudes of these unions.

60. See Bentley B. Gilbert, *The Evolution of National Insurance in Great Britain* (London: Michael Joseph, 1966) chs. 4 and 6 *passim*.

61. Roberts, *The Trades Union Congress*, pp. 127–8.

62. Ibid., Webbs, loc. cit.; Henry Pelling, *A History of British Trade Unionism* (London: Macmillan, 1972) ch. VI.

63. Roberts, *The Trades Union Congress*, p. 128.

64. Rimlinger, *Welfare Policy and Industrialisation*, pp. 194–5. For benefits provided by the unions locally and for mutual aid funds in the United States generally see Roy Lubove, *The Struggle for Social Security 1900–1935* (Cambridge, Mass.; Harvard University Press, 1968) pp. 17–22.

65. Greenstone, *Labor in American Politics*, pp. 41–5; Bagwell and Mingay, *Britain and America 1850–1939*, pp. 210–11.

66. Greenstone, ibid., pp. 45–6.

67. While industrial unrest generally and various protest movements, e.g. the 'Townsend movement' of old people, must be held as an important indirect influence on the social security legislation of the New Deal there was no direct pressure from organised labour for large-scale state intervention. In the post-war years too, medicare and other anti-poverty programmes seem more a reaction to urban disorder, civil rights and liberal protest movements than a response to pressure from labour. On these points see Rimlinger, *Welfare Policy and Industrialisation*, pp. 200–5; Frances Fox Piven and Richard A. Cloward, *Regulating the Poor* (London: Tavistock, 1972) Parts I and II; Theodore R. Marmor, *The Politics of Medicare* (London: Routledge, 1970).

68. See p. 72 above.

69. Rimlinger, *Welfare Policy and Industrialisation*, p. 249; Reinhard Bendix, *Work and Authority in Industry* (Los Angeles: University of California Press, 1974) pp. 185–90.

70. Apart from pensions for certain classes of government employees and a mutual aid association system for certain other public employees, the main social security provision was health insurance (begun in 1922) for workers in large enterprises of selected industries. The war years saw a substantial expansion of all three schemes and the beginning of several new schemes including insurance pensions. Post-war reforms under the allied occupation (SCAP) laid the foundations of a comprehensive system of social security and labour legislation. See George F. Rohrlich, 'War and Postwar Developments in Japanese Social Security', *Bulletin of the International Social Security Association*, III (July 1950); Kazuo Okochi, *Labor in Modern Japan* (Tokyo: The Science Council of Japan, 1958).

71. See for example Hirschmeier and Yui, *Development of Japanese Business*, pp. 80, 96–9.

72. Okochi, *Labor in Modern Japan*; Matsushima, 'Labour Management Relations in Japan' in *Japanese Sociological Studies*, pp. 78–80.

73. See Heidenheimer, *British Journal of Political Science*; Lubove, *The Struggle For Social Security*, pp. 57–9, 62–5, 86–7; Marmor, *The Politics of Medicare*, p. 26 for examples of entrenched opposition to social security programmes.

74. Gilbert, *The Evolution of National Insurance in Great Britain*, p. 165.

75. Karl Marx 'The Eighteenth Brumaire of Louis Bonaparte' in *Marx and Engels – Basic Writings*, ed. Lewis S. Feuer (London: Collins/Fontana, 1969) p. 360.

76. On the determinants of state welfare see Pryor, *Public Expenditures*; Wilensky, *The Welfare State and Equality*; Koji Taira and Peter Kilby, 'Differences in Social Security Development in Selected Countries', *International Social Security Review*, vol. 22(2), 1969; Henry Aaron 'Social Security: International Comparison' in *Studies in the Economics of Income Maintenance*, ed. Otto Eckstein (Washington D.C.: Brookings Institute, 1967).

77. See A. L. Webb and J. E. B. Sieve, *Income Redistribution and the Welfare State* (London: Bell, 1971). For West Germany and

Norway see *Incomes in Post-War Europe* (Geneva: United Nations, 1967) ch. 6, pp. 30–5.

78. Webb and Sieve, ibid., ch. 7.

79. *Incomes in Post-War Europe*, ch. 1, pp. 15–16; ch. 6, p. 41. See however, Organisation for Economic Co-operation and Development (O.E.C.D.), *Education, Inequality and Lifechances,* vols. 1 and 2 (Paris; 1975) for more optimistic assessments of the redistributive effect of taxation and social services. It should be noted that studies of income redistribution generally refer to transfer between income groups or units rather than occupational/social class groups.

80. J. L. Nicholson, *Redistribution of Income in the United Kingdom* (London: Bowes and Bowes, 1964) p. 61.

81. Titmuss, *Income Distribution and Social Change.*

82. Ibid.

83. David Harvey, *Social Justice and the City* (London: Edward Arnold, 1975) p. 294.

84. Frank Field, *Unequal Britain* (London: Hutchinson, 1974) pp. 9–13; A. H. Halsey (ed.), *Trends in British Society since 1900* (London: Macmillan, 1972) p. 343.

85. See Graham Kalton, *The Public Schools* (London: Longmans Green, 1966); Howard Glennerster and Richard Pryke, *The Public Schools* (London: Fabian Society, 1966); Halsey, ibid., pp. 160–2, 170, 187.

86. Halsey, ibid., pp. 161–2, 182, 189. However, more recent data on higher education show an appreciable narrowing of class differentials in Britain and other Western countries. See O.E.C.D., *Education, Inequality & Lifechances*, vol. 1, pp. 168–70, 541.

87. This seems particularly true of the lower working-class people who had no provision in the form of friendly society or trade union benefits or other savings. On the other hand there is little doubt that the middle classes have also benefitted from the development of state pensions (and public sector occupational pensions), especially after the Second World War. How far class differences in the life-chances of the old have narrowed since the turn of the century and what part the welfare state may have played in it are questions that cannot, of course, be settled without a great deal of research.

88. See for example, John Saville 'The Welfare State: An Historical Approach', *New Reasoner*, vol. 3, 1957–8; Robin Blackburn, 'The Unequal Society', in *Power in Britain*, ed. John Urry and John

Wakeford (London: Heinemann, 1973); John Westergaard and Henrietta Resler, *Class in a Capitalist Society: A Study of Contemporary Britain* (London: Heinemann, 1975) esp. Part Two (ch. 4), Part Three (ch. 3) and Part Five.

89. This seems to me to be the case albeit this judgement does scant justice to the sophistication, elegance and originality of recent contributions to stratification analysis. See for example J. H. Goldthorpe, 'Social Stratification in Industrial Society' in *Class Status and Power*, ed. Reinhard Bendix and Seymour Martin Lipset (London: Routledge, 1967); Frank Parkin, *Class Inequality and Political Order* (London: Paladin, 1972), and Anthony Giddens, *The Class Structure of the Advanced Societies* (London: Hutchinson, 1973). Theorists with an industrial society perspective on class have, however, shown greater awareness of the significance of the welfare state. See for example Ralf Dahrendorf, *Class and Class Conflict in Industrial Society* (London: Routledge, 1959) pp. 61–4 and his 'Recent Changes in the Class Structure of European Societies', *Daedalus* 93, Winter 1964, p. 239.

90. Some of the implications of the development of welfare for class theory are examined in S. M. Miller and Pamela Roby, 'Poverty: Changing Social Stratification' in *The Concept of Poverty*, ed. Peter Townsend (London: Heinemann, 1970).

91. A part of the problem seems to arise out of sociologists' use of the term 'market' in a neo-Weberian sense, i.e. to denote the economic ('market situation') as distinct from the social ('status situation') position. This usage perhaps obscures the fact that the 'market situation' of groups can be determined by market as well as non-market forces.

92. Karl Marx and Friedrich Engels, 'Manifesto of the Communist Party', in Feuer, *Marx and Engels*, p. 51.

93. T. B. Bottomore and Maximilien Rubel (eds), *Karl Marx: Selected Writings* (Harmondsworth: Penguin, 1969) p. 190.

94. Westergaard and Resler, *Class in a Capitalist Society*, p. 178.

95. Lewis A. Coser, *The Functions of Social Conflict* (London: Routledge, 1956).

96. See for example D. V. Donnison and others, *Social Policy and Administration* (London: Allen and Unwin, 1965) pp. 20–3. Studies of particular professions have also rarely made the effect of the development of the social services on the profession a focal point of analysis. See for example Brian Abel-Smith, *A History of the Nursing*

Profession (London: Heinemann, 1960); Asher Tropp, *The School Teachers* (London: Heinemann, 1957).

97. See Adrian Sinfield, *Which Way for Social Work?* (London: Fabian Society, 1969); Peter Leonard, 'Professionalization, Community Action and the growth of Social Service Bureaucracies' in *Professionalisation and Social Change: Sociological Review Monograph No. 20*, ed. Paul Halmos (University of Keele, 1973).

98. Titmuss, *Commitment to Welfare*, p. 241.

99. Titmuss, *Essays on the Welfare State*, pp. 159–60, 162–4. This is also suggested by the data in the *Report of the Royal Commission on Doctors' and Dentists' Remuneration 1957–1960*, Cmd. 939, H.M.S.O. 1960 pp. 30, 40, 42–4 and Guy Routh, *Occupation and Pay in Great Britain* 1906–60 (Cambridge: Cambridge University Press, 1965) p. 63; Noel and Jose Parry, *The Rise of the Medical Profession* (London: Croom Helm, 1976) pp. 192–3, 198, 212, 222–3.

100. Titmuss, *Commitment to Welfare*, p. 237; *Essays on the Welfare State* pp. 165–9; Terence J. Johnson, *Professions and Power* (London: Macmillan, 1972) p. 53; Stephen Hatch, *Towards Participation in Local Services* (London: Fabian Society, 1973) p. 9; Parry and Parry, *The Rise of the Medical Profession*, pp. 147–52, 192–3, 212.

101. For some recent developments in this area see the Open University, *Whose Schools?* (Milton Keynes: Open University Press, 1974) Part 2; David Phillips 'Community Health Councils' in *The Year Book of Social Policy in Britain 1974*, ed. Kathleen Jones (London: Routledge, 1975).

102. See Elihu Katz and Brenda Danet (eds), *Bureaucracy and the Public* (New York: Basic Books, 1973).

103. On the difference between professional and bureaucratic orientations see Peter M. Blau and W. Richard Scott, *Formal Organizations* (London: Routledge, 1963) pp. 60–74; Amitai Etzioni, *Complex Organizations* (Englewood Cliffs: Prentice–Hall, 1964) pp. 76–7 and ch. 9; Katz and Danet, ibid., Part II, esp. pp. 162–6.

104. Blau and Scott, op. cit.; Katz and Danet, op. cit.

105. See for example the Open University, *Community Involvement in Decision Making: Decision-Making in British Education Systems*, (Milton Keynes: Open University Press, 1974) pp. 18–9, 35–6; Hatch, *Towards Participation*, pp. 10–11, 15.

106. For example, on the social background of the members of

regional hospital boards and hospital management committees, which
were responsible for the administration of hospital services until
recently (1974), see Mary Stewart, *Unpaid Public Service* (London:
Fabian Society, 1964), and *Public Service for the Community* (London: Fabian Society, 1969) by the same author.

107. The Open University, *Community Involvement in Decision Making*, esp. pp. 29–32; see also Stewart, ibid.

Chapter Seven

1. This chapter draws on Ramesh Mishra, 'Convergence Theory and Social Change: The development of Welfare in Britain and the Soviet Union', *Comparative Studies in Society and History*, vol. 18(1), Jan 1976.

2. Marx wrote little directly about the social organisation (including the nature of distribution) of the future (socialist) society. The basic Marxian text on the subject sketches the barest outline of the nature of socialist distribution. See the 'Critique of the Gotha Programme' in Lewis S. Feuer (ed.), *Marx and Engels: Basic Writings* (London: Fontana/Collins, 1969) ch. V. However, despite varying pronouncements and interpretations by Soviet and other Marxists on the subject, the idea of distribution based largely on need and modelled on collective consumption remains pivotal to Marxian socialism.

3. Karl Marx 'Critique of the Gotha Programme', Feuer, *Marx and Engels: Basic Writings*, pp. 156–61. The notion of a transitional period between capitalism and communism has been the subject of a great deal of debate and controversy. See for example, E. Mandel, *Marxist Economic Theory* (London: Merlin, 1974) chs. 15 and 17; Paul M. Sweezy and Charles Bettelheim, *On the Transition to Socialism* (New York: Monthly Review Press, 1972).

4. For Britain see J. C. Kincaid, *Poverty and Equality in Britain* (Harmondsworth: Penguin, 1973) p. 106. For the U.S.S.R. see United Nations, *Incomes in Post-War Europe* (Geneva: 1967) ch. 9, p. 5; Robert J. Osborn, *Soviet Social Policies* (Homewood, Ill.: Dorsey, 1970) p. 34.

5. J. Wilczynski, *The Economics of Socialism* (London: Allen and Unwin, 1970) pp. 154–7.

6. There is no child tax allowance. Bachelors and childless couples

pay a slightly higher rate of tax than families. See Osborn, *Soviet Social Policies*.

7. *Incomes in Post-War Europe*, ch. 11, p. 8; ch. 9, p. 34.

8. Alexander S. Balinky, 'Non-housing Objectives of Soviet Housing Policy', *Problems of Communism*, vol. 10(4), Jul–Aug. 1961, p. 21.

9. Michael Gamarnikow, *Economic Reforms in Eastern Europe* (Detroit: Wayne State University Press, 1968) pp. 65–72.

10. Alex Inkeles, 'Social Stratification and Mobility in the Soviet Union', in *Class, Status, and Power*, ed. Reinhard Bendix and Seymour Martin Lipset (London: Routledge, 1968) p. 520.

11. Osborn, *Soviet Social Policies*, pp. 81–2, 73.

12. Ibid., pp. 82–4.

13. Donald D. Barry, 'Housing in the U.S.S.R.', *Problems of Communism*, vol. 18(3), May–June 1969, p. 10.

14. See for example Bernice Q. Madison, *Social Welfare in the Soviet Union* (Stanford: Stanford University Press, 1968) ch. 6 *passim* and pp. 25, 188–90, 215.

15. See Nigel Grant, *Soviet Education* (Harmondsworth: Penguin, 1968) chs. 2–4.

16. Gordon Hyde, *The Soviet Health Service* (London: Lawrence and Wishart, 1974) pp. 125–6.

17. Mark G. Field, *Doctor and Patient in Soviet Russia* (Cambridge, Mass.: Harvard University Press, 1957) pp. 184–5.

18. Barry, *Problems of Communism*, p. 8; Osborn, *Soviet Social Policies*, p. 63.

19. Barry, ibid., pp. 2–3, 5; T. Sosnovy 'Housing Conditions and Urban Development in the U.S.S.R.', U.S. Congress Joint Economic Committee, *New Directions in the Soviet Economy, Part IIB* (Washington: U.S. Govt Printing Office, 1966) p. 545; *Statistical Year Book 1974* (New York: United Nations, 1975), Table 204 (Summary of housing conditions).

20. See U.S. Department of Health, Education and Welfare, *Report on Social Security Programme in the Soviet Union* (Washington D.C.: 1960) pp. 107–11; Frederic L. Pryor, *Public Expenditures in Communist and Capitalist Nations* (London: Allen and Unwin, 1968) p. 144.

21. Osborn, *Soviet Social Policies*, p. 91; Hyde, *The Soviet Health Service*, p. 125.

22. Richard M. Titmuss, *The Gift Relationship* (Harmondsworth: Penguin, 1973), pp. 199–201.

23. Grant, *Soviet Education*, pp. 75–6, 83; Osborn, *Soviet Social Policies*, pp. 58–61, 92–3.

24. Madison, *Social Welfare in the Soviet Union*, pp. 56–7, 60–1, 206–8, 220–1. Despite the 'anti-familial' ideology of Marxism, Soviet law recognises quite wide kinship relations as far as obligation to support kin is concerned. See, for example, Osborn, ibid., p. 70.

25. Mervyn Matthews, *Class and Society in Soviet Russia* (London: Allen Lane, 1972) p. 88.

26. Bernice Madison, 'Soviet Income Maintenance Policy for the 1970s', *Journal of Social Policy*, vol. 2(2), Apr 1973, pp. 109–10.

27. See Madison, *Social Welfare in the Soviet Union*, pp. 207, 220–1.

28. David Lane, *The End of Inequality? Stratification under state socialism* (Harmondsworth: Penguin, 1971) p. 69; P. J. D. Wiles and Stefan Markowski, 'Income Distribution Under Communism and Capitalism' (in two parts), *Soviet Studies*, vol. 22(3), Jan 1971, p. 344.

29. See for example Frank Parkin, *Class Inequality and Political Order* (London: Paladin, 1972) pp. 118, 144.

30. Lane, *The End of Inequality?*, pp. 106–16.

31. Gaston V. Rimlinger, *Welfare Policy and Industrialization in Europe, America, and Russia* (New York: John Wiley, 1971) p. 258.

32. Field, *Doctor and Patient in Soviet Russia*, pp. 16–7, 28.

33. Seymour M. Rosen, *Education and Modernisation in the U.S.S.R.* (Reading, Mass.: Addison-Wesley, 1971) p. 32.

34. Balinky, *Problems of Communism*, pp. 17–8; T. Sosnovy, 'The Soviet Housing Situation Today', *Soviet Studies*, vol. 11(1), Jul 1959, p. 1.

35. Rimlinger, *Welfare Policy and Industrialisation*, pp. 300–1.

36. Ibid., pp. 258–9.

37. Madison, *Social Welfare in the Soviet Union*, p. 52.

38. Rimlinger, *Welfare Policy and Industrialisation*, pp. 265–7.

39. Ibid., pp. 267, 280.

40. Ibid., pp. 274–6, 280, 284; Madison, *Social Welfare in the Soviet Union*, pp. 58–9, 195.

41. Rimlinger, p. 286; Madison, ibid., pp. 195–6.

42. Rimlinger, pp. 285, 290.

43. Ibid., pp. 292–3.

44. Madison, *Journal of Social Policy*.

45. Hyde, *The Soviet Health Service*, ch. 1; Brian Abel-Smith, 'The History of Medical Care' in *Comparative Development in Social Welfare*, ed. E. W. Martin (London: Allen and Unwin, 1972) p. 220.

46. Field, *Doctor and Patient in Soviet Russia*, p. 17.

47. Ibid., pp. 20, 23; Sidney and Beatrice Webb, *Soviet Communism: A New Civilization?* (Private Subscription Edition, Great Britain, 1935) pp. 837, 842, 852–3.

48. Sir Arthur Newsholme and John Adams Kingsbury, *Red Medicine* (New York: Doubleday, 1933) pp. 189, 269–70.

49. Field, *Doctor and Patient in Soviet Russia*, pp. 21–2, 30.

50. Hyde, *The Soviet Health Service*, p. 101.

51. Ibid., pp. 98–101; Field, *Doctor and Patient in Soviet Russia*, pp. 22–3.

52. Alexander Block, 'Soviet Housing: The Historical Aspect', *Soviet Studies*, vol. 3(1), Jul 1951, p. 8.

53. Balinky, *Problems of Communism*, p. 17.

54. Ibid., p. 18.

55. Ibid.; Sosnovy, in *New Directions in the Soviet Economy*, p. 14.

56. See Henry W. Morton, 'What have Soviet leaders done about the housing crisis?' in Henry W. Morton and Rudolf L. Tokes (eds), *Soviet Politics and Society in the 1970s* (New York: Free Press, 1974) pp. 165–8.

57. Sosnovy, in *New Directions in the Soviet Economy*, p. 14.

58. Barry, *Problems of Communism*, p. 10; Morton, in *Soviet Politics and Society in the 1970s*, 180–3.

59. D. V. Donnison, *The Government of Housing* (Harmondsworth: Penguin, 1967) pp. 140–4.

60. Rosen, *Education & Modernisation in the U.S.S.R.*, p. 32.

61. Ibid., p. 38.

62. Nicholas De Witt, *Education and Professional Employment in the U.S.S.R.* (Washington D.C.: National Science Foundation, U.S. Govt Printing Office, 1961) pp. 80–1.

63. Ibid., p. 82; Rosen, *Education and Modernisation in the U.S.S.R.*, p. 39.

64. Rosen, ibid., p. 40.

65. Ibid., p. 32.

66. Ibid., pp. 38, 82–3; De Witt, *Education & Professional*

Employment in the U.S.S.R., p. 66.

67. De Witt, ibid., p. 65.

68. Ibid.

69. Osborn, *Soviet Social Policies*, pp. 95–108; Grant, *Soviet Education*, pp. 96–103.

70. Grant, ibid., pp. 98, 103. By the mid-1970s over 80 per cent of the Soviet children were said to be completing the ten year school. See *Socialism: Theory and Practice* (Moscow) Jan. 1976, p. 106.

71. Parkin, *Class Inequality and Political Order*, pp. 166, 110; Mervyn Matthews, *Class and Society in Soviet Russia* (London: Allen Lane, Penguin, 1972) pp. 291, 297; A. H. Halsey (ed.), *Trends in British Society since 1900* (London: Macmillan, 1972) pp. 182–3, 190–1; Alex Inkeles and Raymond A. Bauer, *The Soviet Citizen* (Cambridge, Mass.: Harvard University Press, 1959) pp. 142–4. More recent evidence, however, suggests that advanced capitalist countries may be 'catching up'. See Organisation for Economic Co-operation and Development (O.E.C.D.), *Education, Inequality and Life Chances*, 2 vols (Paris: 1975), vol. I, pp. 168–70; vol. 2, pp. 163–9, 177–9.

72. Parkin, *Class Inequality and Political Order*, pp. 148–9; G. V. Osipov (ed.), *Industry and Labour in the U.S.S.R.* (London: Tavistock, 1966) pp. 126–9.

73. Parkin, ibid., p. 142; Lane, *The End of Inequality?*, p. 94; Matthews, *Class and Society in Soviet Russia*, pp. 292–5, 302–5.

74. Lane, *The End of Inequality?*, pp. 111–6; Matthews, *Class and Society in Soviet Russia*, pp. 265, 291, 297.

75. See pp. 95 and 126 above. For figures on expenditure including housing see J. F. Sleeman, *The Welfare State* (London: Allen and Unwin, 1973) p. 136.

76. See Harry G. Shaffer (ed.), *The Soviet Economy* (London: Methuen, 1964) pp. 82, 85–6, 103.

77. See J. Wilczynski, *Socialist Economic Development and Reforms* (London: Macmillan, 1972) ch. 7 *passim* and Naum Jasny, 'Plan and Superplan' in *The Soviet Economy*, ed. Shaffer.

78. See Murray Yanowitch, 'The Soviet Income Revolution', *Slavic Review*, vol. 22(4), Dec 1963; Parkin, *Class Inequality and Political Order*, pp. 118–20, 144; Wilczynski, *The Economics of Socialism*, p. 106.

79. Wilczynski, ibid., pp. 109–10.

80. *Incomes in Post-War Europe*, ch. 11, pp. 7–8.

81. Ibid.; Wiles and Markowski, (Part 2), *Soviet Studies*, vol. 22(4), Apr 1971, pp. 508, 511; Philip Hanson, *The Consumer in the Soviet Economy* (London: Macmillan, 1968) pp. 72–4.

82. Lane, *The End of Inequality?*, p. 77; Matthews, *Class and Society in Soviet Russia*, p. 227; Balinky, in *Problems of Communism*, p. 20. See also Paul Halmos (ed.), *Hungarian Sociological Studies: Sociological Review Monograph No. 17* (University of Keele, 1972) pp. 282–3, 47–8.

83. Halmos, ibid., pp. 47–8, 285–6, 292–3.

84. Inkeles and Bauer, *The Soviet Citizen*. This study, one of several arising out of the Harvard Project on the Soviet Social System, was based on written questionnaires completed by nearly 3 000 Soviet emigrés supplemented with over 700 interviews held during 1950–1 (ibid., pp. vii, 5).

85. Ibid., p. 236.

86. Ibid., p. 238.

87. Ibid., p. 242.

88. Herbert Marcuse, *One Dimensional Man* (London: Sphere Books, 1968) pp. 52–7.

89. Parkin, *Class Inequality and Political Order*, pp. 175–8; Francois Fejto, *A History of the People's Democracies* (Harmondsworth: Penguin, 1974) pp. 396–9.

90. Field, *Doctor and Patient in Soviet Russia*, p. 18; Hyde, *The Soviet Health Service*, pp. 290–2.

91. Hyde, ibid., pp. 288–9; John Fry, *Medicine in Three Societies* (Aylesbury, Bucks: M.T.P., 1969) ch. 7.

92. See for example, Madison, *Journal of Social Policy*, pp. 89, 94–6.

93. This is suggested by the fact that red tape and bureaucratism are rarely mentioned as problems arising out of the delivery of education and health services in either of the two countries. Personal experience of the services also supports the view that the nature of the service in question is an important factor.

94. See for example Richard C. Gripp, *The Political System of Communism* (London: Nelson, 1973) ch. 5; Jerry F. Hough 'Political Participation in the Soviet Union', *Soviet Studies* vol. 28(1), Jan 1976.

95. Osborn, *Soviet Social Policies*, p. 86; Madison, *Journal of Social Policy*, pp. 90–2, 97–8, 130–1; Hyde, *Soviet Health Service*,

pp. 77, 199–200.

96. Madison, ibid., pp. 133–4; Grant, *Soviet Education*, 59–63. For Parent-Teacher Associations and other forms of parental involvement in British schools see the Open University, 'Community Involvement in Decision-Making' in *Decision-Making in British Educational Systems* (Milton Keynes: Open University Press, 1974) pp. 16–21; Anne Sharrock, *Home-School Relations* (London: Macmillan, 1970) esp. ch. 3. In the United States, however, parental contact and involvement with schools is much greater than in Britain (the Open University, ibid.).

97. Madison, ibid., p. 99; Grant, ibid., p. 61.

98. Matthews, *Class and Society in Soviet Russia*, pp. 239–42; Murray Yanowitch and Wesley A. Fisher (eds), *Social Stratification and Mobility in the U.S.S.R.* (New York: International Arts and Sciences, 1973) pp. 83, 98–9.

99. On the U.S.S.R. see Osborn, *Soviet Social Policies*, pp. 257–9; Jack Miller, *Life in Russia Today* (London: Batsford, 1969) pp. 100–2. On Britain see Stephen Hatch (ed.), *Towards Participation in Local Services* (London: Fabian Society, 1973) pp. 35–42.

100. Gabriel A. Almond and G. Bingham Powell, Jr., *Comparative Politics* (Boston: Little, Brown, 1966) p. 273.

101. Needless to say we refer to dissimilarities that are closely related to welfare. As regards more general contrasts relevant to the well-being of the people, e.g. concerning civil, intellectual and political liberties, rule of law, etc., we have said little. This does not in any way imply that they are unimportant.

Concluding Remarks

1. For the leading ideas of Ivan Illich see his *Tools for Conviviality* (London: Calder and Boyars, 1973); *Deschooling Society* (Harmondsworth: Penguin, 1973); *Medical Nemesis* (London: Calder and Boyars, 1975); *Energy and Equity* (London: Calder and Boyars, 1974).

2. Richard M. Titmuss, *Essays on the Welfare State* (London: Allen and Unwin, 1963) pp. 23–4, 27–8.

3. See Illich, *Deschooling Society* and *Medical Nemesis*.

4. Illich, *Tools for Conviviality*, pp. 24–6.

5. Ibid., ch. II.

Index